HOTEL DESIGN

INTERNATIONAL PORTFOLIO OF THE FINEST CONTEMPORARY DESIGNS

Rockport Publishers, Rockport, Massachusetts

BOOK DEVELOPMENT AND EDITORIAL
ROSALIE M. GRATTAROTI

BOOK DESIGN
LAURA HERRMANN

DESIGN AND PRODUCTION
SARA DAY

COVER DESIGN
SARA DAY

PRODUCTION MANAGER
BARBARA STATES

PRODUCTION ASSISTANT
PAT O'MALEY

First published in the United States of America by:
Rockport Publishers, Inc.
146 Granite Street
Rockport, Massachusetts 01966
Fax: (508)546-7141

Distributed to the book trade in the United States by:
Consortium Book Sales and Distribution
1045 Westgate Drive
Saint Paul, MN 55114-0165
1-800-283-3572

ISBN 1-56496-221-0

5 7 9 10 8 6 4

Printed in Hong Kong

CONTENTS

THE HOTEL AS GLOBAL VILLAGE

By Justin Henderson

In the last ten years the hotel business came of age as a multi-national global entity. To one carefully observing from the sidelines (I've been writing on hotel design for most of those ten years) it appears as if hotel developers—of chains, groups, franchises, and independents alike—finally have tuned in to the elements that add up to success in the brave new world of international hospitality. Perhaps the most critical of those elements is design, for all kinds of reasons—most of which pertain to the increasing sophistication, and therefore raised expectations, of contemporary travelers. Whether a beautiful hotel on every beach in the world is a sign of progress is debatable, but there is little doubt that an ecologically sensitive low-rise building, incorporating motifs drawn from local architectural styles, is, in most contexts, preferable to an urban-style high rise casting long shadows across the beach.

This respect for context and scale is emblematic of a general trend, in which architects and designers have tuned in to the more modest, culturally-sensitive imperatives of the 1990s, and instituted honest style and real substance. Which is not to deny the luxurious or the fantastic as critical elements: world-class cities demand world-class luxury hotels, and likewise there is perhaps no more theatrical, fantasy-laden architectural confection than a resort hotel, say, in close proximity to an international theme park. The point is appropriateness—in the city, elegant, traditional style fits—but not everybody wants to put on a tie for dinner in a beach front resort.

Linking old and new, local village with global village, region with region and nation with nation, are the new hotels of the world, some of which are showcased on these pages. The architects and designers who have created these properties are engaged in the invention of a new international style of hospitality design —one which sustains a high level of comfort and technology to attract the tourists of the west, but which does so without abandoning or ignoring the indigenous cultures of host nations or regions. The pursuit of Western-style comfort should not turn every hotel into a theme park decorated with the trappings of place but lacking the unique substance of that place. The real challenge—and it has been met in many of the hotels featured here—is to give the tourist the comfort level they expect in an

honest cultural context. Likewise, in the urban business hotel, the much-traveled international businessperson would rather deal with the familiar instead of the unknown—but, again, it is the responsibility—and what a wonderful opportunity!—of the designer and developer to utilize local artifacts, fabrics, foods, and style, without making the traveler pay too much of a price for a touch of authenticity.

Our featured properties, from Korea to Bophthatswana, from Kirkland, Washington to West Palm Beach, Florida, demonstrate that designers around the world have responded to the demands of short-term vacationers, heavily-traveled businessmen, meeting planners, and conventioneers with hotel designs that manage to play to every segment of an increasingly diverse market. Diverse, and as I mentioned before, sophisticated. This sophistication—the international traveler's heightened awareness of the architectural and interior design styles of a dozen different cultures—is a gift the hotel architects and designers have given to today's travelers, who have become knowledgeable in the art and design of the countries to which they travel simply by paying attention to the furniture, crafts, and works of art that have been integrated into these hotels. And so, in addition to the rich, honest regionalism which inspires the architecture of many of these hotels, designers con make reference to Venice in Florida, or Rome in California, or Greece in Australia, and know that guests will feel utterly at home in the lobbies and restaurants and gathering places in their hotels, transplanted thousands of miles and hundreds of years by visual reference, but connected, by fax, phone, and the ubiquitous CNN, to the present-day world.

Another big step has been the introduction of one or more restaurants designed for both guests and non-guests, particularly in urban hotels. In addition to establishing another outlet for design creativity—one which permits the designer to stray, in many cases, from the general motifs of the hotel interior into exploring other themes—these new hotel restaurants have liberated guests from the often-boring and almost always uninspired designs (and menus) of the old-style standard hotel coffee shop. Now, diversity is the key, as architects build in separate street entrances for restaurants, and designers employ historical, regional, international, and other sources as inspiration for food service outlets ranging from three meal coffee shops to four star high end dining rooms that actually attract non-guests in for meals.

The visual evidence on these pages richly demonstrates another important aspect of contemporary hotel design: the guest room. These days, guest rooms are actually designed with specific attention to the comfort of —The Guest! Amazing what a little competition can do! Hotels haven't always had non-smoking floors, or concierge levels with private check-in, or in-room fax lines and computer outlets. From richer fabrics on beds and furniture, to multiple telephones, marble bathrooms, ample closets and built-in hair dryers, the hotel rooms of the 1990s—as is vividly illustrated herein—are wonderfully comfortable places, sanctuaries for the traveler in search of peace, solitude, and a place to relax—or work, if work needs doing.

The next wave of exciting hotels will be opening, I venture to predict, in a host of new markets: the Pacific Rim will continue to expand to meet the demands of the new multi-national marketplace with urban properties in prospering cities as well as resorts dotting the literally thousands of islands out there; South America and Africa will emerge as vacation destinations for those sophisticates who feel they have already covered Europe and the Pacific; and finally, there is Eastern Europe and Russia. With all their difficulties, those countries are rich in culture and history, and have much to offer. Look for all the major international hotel groups to expand into all those markets, as well as continually upgrading and opening properties in the more predictable regions of the United States and Europe. Wherever new hotels open, in order to succeed they will have to meet the high standards of architecture and design which have been established over the last few years by the designers whose work is featured in these pages..

—Justin Henderson

A resident of Seattle, Washington, Justin Henderson is a Senior Editor with Interiors *magazine, and has been writing about hotel and restaurant design since 1984.*

FISHER ISLAND CLUBHOUSE
Fisher Island, Florida
*An old airplane hangar from
the original Vanderbilt estate
on Fisher Island was converted
into the luxurious yet functional
Spa Internazionale.*

FISHER ISLAND CLUBHOUSE
Fisher Island, Florida
*The historical character of the original
facade was successfully preserved at
the Spa Internazionale while the
interior was transformed with rich,
new materials and unique amenities.*

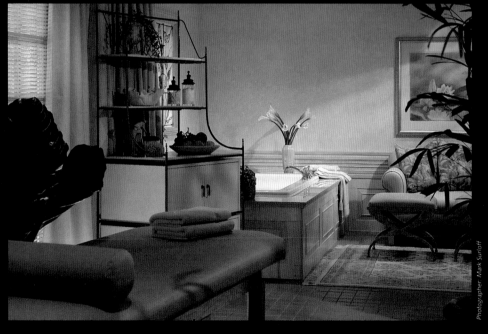

Photographer: Mark Surloff

SHERATON BAL HARBOUR
Bal Harbour, Florida
*An exciting new concept, a
"Marketessen," was created
for this hotel.*

CAROLE KORN INTERIORS, INC.

622 Banyan Trail, Boca Raton, Florida 33431
407/997-2888, Fax: 407/997-2297

CAROLE KORN INTERIORS

Carole Korn Interiors has been creating award-winning designs for the hospitality industry for more than 20 years. In the past year alone, Carole Korn Interiors earned more than 40 prestigious awards for design excellence. The firm, which has been ranked as one of the top ten interior design firms in the United States, was honored with Gold Key Awards from the American Hotel & Motel Association in three of the past five years. ▭ As a 50-member, $50 million-a-year firm, Carole Korn Interiors has the talent and experience to ensure that each job is completed on time and within budget. From lobbies to restaurants, guest rooms to ballrooms, Carole Korn Interiors consistently produces outstanding designs that increase revenues while appealing to guests. ▭ Recently, Carole Korn Interiors completed the $22 million renovation of the Sheraton Bal Harbour in Bal Harbour, Florida. Other clients include Hilton, Ramada, and The Registry Hotels. ▭ Carole Korn, president and founder of Carole Korn Interiors, is one of only 4 interior designers in the United States to have earned the designation of Master Hotel Supplier.

PALM BEACH
AIRPORT HILTON
West Palm Beach, Florida
The private dining room was given an eclectic design, making it appropriate for business meetings or parties.

Photographer: Todd Dyess

Photographer: Todd Dyess

SHERATON BAL HARBOUR
Bal Harbour, Florida
The columns at the entrance to the Garden Cafe are designed to create a casual, inviting, and dramatic atmosphere.

SHERATON BAL HARBOUR
Bal Harbour, Florida
Instead of a typical hotel coffee shop, a Garden Cafe concept with a versatile buffet line was created. The restaurant serves guests equally well for breakfast or for lunch and, with the addition of tablecloths and candles, for a casual dinner.

SHERATON BAL HARBOUR
Bal Harbour, Florida
The Bar and Grille features an exhibition kitchen where steaks and seafood are prepared to order in full view of the guests. The woodplank flooring is perfect for dancing and offers the option of additional cocktail or dining space.

FISHER ISLAND CLUBHOUSE
Fisher Island, Florida
Mahogany, leather and verde marble combine to create an upscale bar that appeals to the international guests and residents of Fisher Island.

Photographer: Dan Forer

FISHER ISLAND CLUBHOUSE
Fisher Island, Florida
For continental dining, an elegant dining room was created.

Photographer: Seth Benson

Current and Recent Projects

Four Seasons Wailea Resort
Wailea, Maui, Hawaii

The Four Seasons Biltmore
Santa Barbara, California

Alpha Izu Resort & Spa
Izu, Japan

Alpha Venetian Resort
Gold Coast, Australia

Thanos Hotel at Polis
Island of Cyprus

The Hapuna Beach Hotel
Island of Hawaii

Los Angeles Airport Hilton
 and Towers
Los Angeles, California

The Hyatt Irvine
Irvine, California

Marina Center Marriott
Singapore

DORAL TELLURIDE
Telluride, Colorado

THE OCEAN GRAND HOTEL
Palm Beach, Florida

**THE PENINSULA
BEVERLY HILLS HOTEL**
Beverly Hills, California

JAMES NORTHCUTT ASSOCIATES

717 North La Cienega Boulevard, Los Angeles, California 90069
310/659-8595, Fax: 310/659-7120

JAMES NORTHCUTT ASSOCIATES

A skillful attention to structure, furnishings and details has brought international acclaim to James Northcutt Associates' approach to hotel, resort and country club design. Every project undertaken by the firm is done so with the intention of elevating hotel design to a higher level of excellence, in a style that is both unique and appropriate to the project and environment. Augmenting the practice's diverse experience in architecture and interior design is a scrupulous and creative eye for detail, including a harmonious blending of traditional and contemporary furnishings, the use of distinctive artwork as focal points, and the strategic use of lighting. Providing the client with a total design concept extends even to the coordination of interior plantscape, china, crystal, flat-ware, graphics, menus and uniforms. The result is invariably an environment with an understated elegance that has become the signature style of James Northcutt Associates.

**THE PENINSULA
BEVERLY HILLS HOTEL**
Beverly Hills, California

**LAS MISIONES GOLF
AND COUNTRY CLUB**
Monterrey, Mexico

▌ SURF AND SAND
Laguna Beach, California

▌ THE WILSHIRE
Los Angeles, California

▌ THE OCEAN GRAND HOTEL
Palm Beach, Florida

▌ SURF AND SAND
Laguna Beach, California

13

BRYSON HOTEL
Melbourne, Australia
Influenced by its location
in the heart of Melbourne's
Arts and Theatre district, is
a typical guest room.

BRYSON HOTEL
Melbourne, Australia
The foyer of the 366-room
hotel recreates the ambience
of a classic, refined Victorian
gentlemen's club.

PACIFIC DESIGN GROUP

Australia		Jakarta:	Hong Kong:	Fiji:
Sydney:	Gold Coast:	Suite 09/05, Wisma Bank Dharmala	1701 Hennessy House	PO Box 14465
343 Pacific Highway	Suite 7 2-4 Elliot Street	J.l Jend Sudirman Kav.28	313 Hennessy Road	73 Gordon Street
CROWS NEST NSW 2065	Bundall QLD 4217	Jakarta 12910	Wanchai, Hong Kong	Suva
612/929-0922, Fax: 612/923-2558	075/38-4499, Fax 075/38-3847	6221/521-2138/9, Fax: 6221/521-2126	852, 834-7404, Fax: 852/834-5675	679/303-858, Fax: 679/303-868

PACIFIC DESIGN GROUP

Pacific Design Group is a dynamic design team servicing the hospitality industry, giving their clients personalized attention and excellence of product. The Group brings to every project professional experience in master planning, architecture, interior design and technical operations. ☐ Senior Management involvement in over 300 hospitality projects worldwide adds value to the client's investment through experienced and innovative design. They advance projects by bringing together their valuable network of owners, operators, developers, financiers and contractors. ☐ At Pacific Design Group, an integrated team approach produces creative results that are innovative, rational and cost effective, to satisfy their client's needs and aspirations. Those clients include ITT Sheraton, Hilton International, Radisson Hotels, Accor, Marriott Hotels, Holiday Inns, Rydges Hotel Group, Century Hotels, and many local and regional operators. ☐ Pacific Design Group has two offices in Australia with a network of regional offices in Hong Kong, Singapore, Jakarta, Fiji, Micronesia, and New Zealand. Successful projects for the firm's clients have been completed throughout the Australian, Asian and Pacific region.

HILTON HOTEL
Melbourne, Australia
The grand stair offers a graceful transition between public floors and acts as a visual focal point in the reception area.

CAPITAL HOTEL
Sydney, Australia
*A typical guest room in
this 225-room hotel uses
traditional design with
contemporary fabric colours.*

PLAZA HOTEL AND THE PIER
Cairns, Australia
*Australian native timbers and colours
are used throughout the 220-room
hotel, including the executive lounge.*

RADISSON CENTURY HOTEL
Sydney, Australia
*The lobby lounge of this 291-room hotel
stretches along the contemporary, radiating
form of the ground floor.*

HILTON HOTEL
Melbourne, Australia
The reception area of the 403-room hotel sets new standards in sophisticated elegance.

HILTON HOTEL
Melbourne, Australia
Selected, world-renowned designer retailers have established a specialty shopping arcade within the 403-room hotel.

PLUMERIA RESORT
Saipan, Micronesia
The design of the "raffles theme" enhances the 114-room, seaside resort on the island of Saipan.

NOAHS HOTEL
Christchurch, New Zealand
The award winning Broques Restaurant recreates an authentic European brasserie within the 200-room hotel.

PLUMERIA RESORT
Saipan, Micronesia
*Lounge bar of the
114-room resort. Totally
prefabricated in Australia
and assembled on site.*

NOAHS HOTEL
Christchurch, New Zealand
*The 200-room hotel has been
refurbished to give an international
ambience with a contemporary blend
of European and indigenous products.*

AUCKLAND CLUB
Auckland, New Zealand
This prestigious business club, with its elegant ballroom, is located in the center of Auckland's business district.

HILTON HOTEL
Sydney, Australia
Off the renovated reception area of this 585-room hotel is a warm and intimate lounge area for hotel guests.

HILTON HOTEL
Sydney, Australia
The pre-function area of one of Sydney's largest classical ballrooms within the 585-room hotel.

SHERATON COOK ISLANDS
Cook Islands
The creation of 5 acres of tranquil lagoons
and lush tropical landscaping enhances
the island paradise feeling in this truly
magnificent 200-room resort.

**THE TOWER AT
CENTURY PLAZA**
Los Angeles, California
Lobby

Photographer: Mary E. Nichols

**THE VILLA VERA HOTEL
AND RACQUET CLUB**
Acapulco, Mexico
Dining Terrace

Photographer: Mary E. Nichols

CASTLE PINES GOLF CLUB
Castle Rock, Colorado
*Architecture that is both refined and rustic
allows for a unique approach in scale and
texture of interior furnishings.*

TEXEIRA, INC.

11811 Bellagio Road, Los Angeles, California 90049
310/471-2355, Fax: 310/440-2149

TEXEIRA, INC.

Texeira, Inc. focuses on the essentials, the elements that make up client projects on the basis of form and function:

- The ability to envision and create unique style, balanced by sensible inventiveness.
- A record of fiscal responsibility with regard to project budgets...complex project management experience combined with substantial problem solving capability.
- The capacity to listen and lead with sound visionary ideas...a willingness to take reasonable risks for a sound purpose.

Glenn Texeira's talent for inspiring and influencing his associates and colleagues rewards the client, and all participants involved, by achieving successful results through shared application of ideas, decisions and follow-up. Texeira believes, "Clients hire us not just for 'a look'. Whether it's a classical or avant garde design direction, they can trust the end result to be appropriate to the project's location and marketing position...to be on schedule, within budget, and to remain timeless in function and character." Award winning projects and an impressive client list are testaments to the firm's commitment to client satisfaction and design integrity.

**THE TOWER AT
CENTURY PLAZA
Los Angeles, California**
Sculptural forms, applied finishes, art and artifacts create a contemporary yet classical statement.

Photographer: Mary E. Nichols

THE RITZ CARLTON
Chicago, Illinois

Photographer: Jaime Ardile-Arce

THE PENINSULA, BANGKOK
Bangkok, Thailand
Brennan Beer Gorman/Architects
Texeira, Inc./Interior Design
*An international landmark property on the
Chao Phraya River, setting new standards
of elegance and style in luxury hotel design.*

THE SHERWOOD, TAIPEI
Taipei, Taiwan
*Classical architectural elements and
Asian-influenced furnishings create an
exciting cross-cultural statement.*

Photographer: Charles White

HOTEL BEL AIR
Los Angeles, California
Lush landscaping transforms an exterior corridor into a garden loggia for memorable alfresco dining.

Photographer: Charles White

Photographer: Jaime Ardiles-Arce

HOTEL BEL AIR
Los Angeles, California
By embellishing the best features of the original structure, this extensive renovation retained the casual elegance revered by returning guests.

THE REMINGTON
Houston, Texas
The relaxed ambience of this sunlit dining atrium compléments the adjacent formal restaurant.

Representative List of WAT&G
Hotel Clients
Disney Development Company
Four Seasons Hotels
Hilton Hotels Corporation
Hyatt International Hotels
Inter-Continental Hotel
 Corporation
ITT Sheraton Corporation
Outrigger Hotels Hawaii
Prince Hotels
Prudential Property Company
Ramada International Hotels
Regent International Hotels
The Ritz-Carlton Hotel Company
Shangri-La International
Westin Hotels & Resorts

**SHANGRI-LA HOTEL
GARDEN WING**
Singapore
*The award-winning
165-room addition to
this hotel in Singapore
with its open atrium
lobby, waterfalls and
lush foliage reinforces
Singapore's identity as
"The Garden City."*

THE HOTEL BORA BORA
Tahiti
*This 80-room hotel is designed
as an ancient Tahitian house.
Open-air buildings take advantage of the natural cooling of
the trade winds and merge
modern convenience with
South Seas authenticity.*

WIMBERLY ALLISON TONG & GOO
ARCHITECTS AND PLANNERS

2222 Kalakaua Avenue,
Penthouse
Honolulu, Hawaii 96815
808/922-1253, Fax: 808/922-1250

2260 University Drive
Newport Beach, California 92660
714/574-8500, Fax: 714/574-8550

51 Neil Road, #02-20
Singapore 0208
65/227-2618, Fax: 65/227-0650

Second Floor, Waldron House
57 Old Church Street
London SW3 5BS, England
071/376-3260, Fax: 071/376-3193

BERLY ALLISON TONG & GOO

Tong & Goo is recognized as one of the world's leading firms
otel and resort planning and design. Since its founding in 1945,
npleted work in over 50 countries, with projects throughout the
waii, across the U.S. Mainland, Mexico, South America, the
rope, Africa and the Middle East.

's expertise centers around the planning,
ovation of leisure-oriented facilities, to
ed destination resorts, hotels, condomini-
projects, golf residential communities,
enters, restaurants, clubs and recreational
WAT&G's projects have been widely
prestigious design awards and featured in
tions worldwide. The firm has been rec-
ability to design outstanding facilities
he environment and cultural heritage of
nunity. This sense of place has become
eature of WAT&G projects throughout

FOUR SEASONS HOTEL
Newport Beach, California
*The 222-room, 97-suite, boldly
sculptured hotel occupies a prime
urban site overlooking Newport
Harbor and the Pacific Ocean.*

HILTON HAWAIIAN VILLAGE
Honolulu, Hawaii
This award-winning hotel is the largest and most comprehensive resort in Waikiki.

RAMADA REEF RESORT
Cairns, Australia
This environmentally sensitive 200-room resort was designed to save a dense stand of trees; pools, decks and walkways were all raised to avoid damage to tree roots.

LOS MILLARES GOLF AND COUNTRY CLUB
Spain
Designed in the style of a fishing village with 300 villas creating a unique Andalusian sense of place, this country club is set to open in 1995.

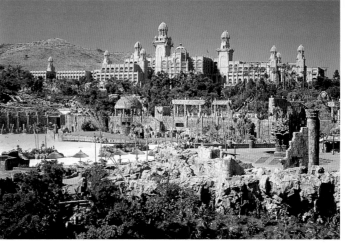

THE PALACE OF THE LOST CITY
Bophuthatswana, Africa
Set amidst lush jungles, waterfalls, and "ruins," this luxury resort hotel was designed to cater to the guests of a mythical king.

GRAND HYATT BALI
Indonesia
This 700-room resort is patterned after fabled Balinese water palaces. Four ethnic villages are set in 40 acres of cascading waterfalls, lush gardens and carp-filled lagoons.

HYATT REGENCY KAUAI
Poipu, Kauai, Hawaii
Sitting on 50 oceanfront acres, this award-winning 600-room Hyatt stretches out among lush gardens and lagoons in traditional Hawaiian architecture.

FOUR SEASONS CHINZAN-SO
Tokyo, Japan
This new 13-story, 286-room hotel is located on the site of a 19th century Shogun's house with rooms overlooking the Shogun's gardens.

THE RITZ-CARLTON HUNTINGTON HOTEL
Pasadena, California
Originally built in 1907 as a world-class resort, this hotel has been meticulously restored and renovated by WAT&G.

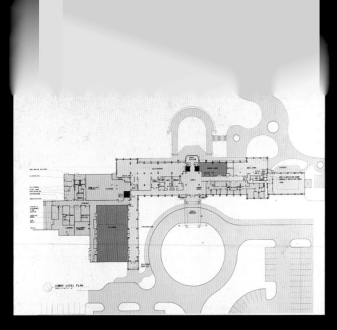

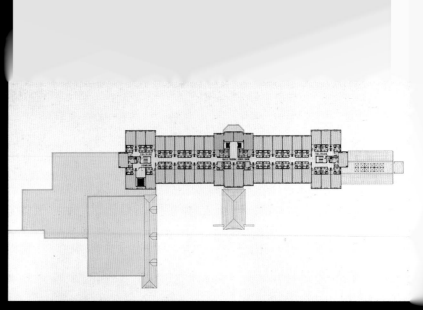

**WASHINGTON DUKE INN
AND GOLF CLUB
Raleigh, North Carolina**
*The gothic-styled facade blends a
steel structure with the existing
architectural style predominant
on the Duke University campus.*

AᵢGROUP/ARCHITECTS, P.C.

1197 Peachtree Street, Atlanta, Georgia 30361

404/873-2555

AiGROUP/ARCHITECTS, P.C.

Established in 1982, AiGroup/Architects, P.C. is a multi-disciplinary design firm serving local, national and international clientele in both the public and private sectors. AiGroup/Architects provides comprehensive full-service architectural design and interior design services, including graphic and product design. Experienced in new construction, as well as refurbishment, renovation, and the repositioning of existing properties, their project list includes office buildings, hotels, conference centers, high-density residential projects, office/industrial parks and specialty retail centers. They have also developed extensive expertise in renovation and expansion of existing properties, including numerous buildings of historical significance. ▭ AiGroup's projects range from the singular small effort to the large scale multi-discipline and complex developments reaching $75,000,000 in cost. ▭ Presently, AiGroup maintains a headquarters office for design and production in Atlanta, as well as an associated office under the name Atelier international in Prague, Czechoslovakia.

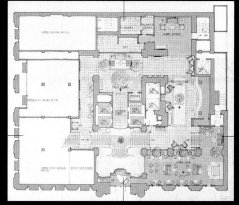

Lobby Level Plan

THE PENINSULA HOTEL
New York, New York
Hotel Lobby
Part of a $50 million historic renovation, the elegant lobby reflects a successful marriage between Art Nouveau and Classic Beaux Arts styling.

RADISSON PLAZA HOTEL @ KALAMAZOO CENTER
Kalamazoo, Michigan

Hotel Motor Court
The addition of a new porte cochere provides the "sense of arrival" needed to enhance the entry. A graceful stepped roofline adds more desirable height and proportion.

Websters Restaurant & Bar
Leaded glass, a featured wine collection, marble floors and rich mahogany millwork highlight this elegant 80 seat dinner atmosphere.

Photographer: Gary Knight & Associates

Photographer: Gary Knight & Associates

Photographer: Gary Knight & Associates

Plaza Cafe
Memorabilia from famous local companies such as the Checker Cab Co. and The Upjohn Company helped to create a playful atmosphere and inspired the architectural detailing in this inviting restaurant.

The Upjohn Suite Bath
Created for the exclusive use of prominent executives, this comfortable bath features warm rich marbles, brass appointments and a jacuzzi bath adjacent to the high style master bedroom.

THE SUITE HOTEL @ UNDERGROUND ATLANTA
Atlanta, Georgia

Dining Room
Original heavy bronze windows frame the delightful view that provides the backdrop for the intimate restaurant elegantly enhanced by exquisite marbles, rich mahogany millwork and hand tufted custom carpets.

Hotel Exterior
The historic five story Connelly Building was preserved, renovated and expanded with the addition of eleven new floors to provide a new 157 room all-suite hotel in Underground Atlanta.

Photographer: Gary Knight & Associates

Photographer: Gary Knight & Associates

Photographer: Gary Knight & Associates

Photographer: Gary Knight & Associates

Standard Suite
Soothing tones of green and rose are accented with the warmth of the rich mahogany casegoods. Commissioned artwork designed especially for each room complements the relaxing residential atmosphere.

Entry
Warm brass accents and the restored original copper canopy provide the desired level of elegance for arriving guests.

TERRA BISTRO, THE VAIL ATHLETIC CLUB
Vail, Colorado
Terra Bistro

Photographer Phillip Nilsson

Photographer Phillip Nilsson

AIELLO ASSOCIATES, INC.

For over thirty years, Aiello Associates has been addressing the challenges of architectural interior design. Accolades attest to the firm's dedication to personal service, attention to detail, their understanding of each client's individual needs and the superior design talent that makes the difference in the ultimate success of each project. ☐ Times have changed and markets have become even more critical to target. Aiello Associates' design teams know how to create effective designs that impact the image, efficiency and bottom line of their clients. Project scope of work spans from high-end full service luxury resorts to restaurants, casinos, entertainment facilities, ski resorts and commercial buildings. ☐ The spirit of teamwork maximizes the exceptional contribution of each member of the firm. Timeless designs, creativity, functionality and value are goals the Aiello design team strives for in each project. ☐ High professional standards ensuring the creation of trust-based relationships is one of the many reasons why Aiello Associates has maintained the respect of its clients and the design community for decades.

BULLWHACKERS GAMING ESTABLISHMENT
Central City, Colorado
Atrium and Grand Staircase

Photographer Ed Lacasse

Restaurant entry and view of
custom mural by Carlo Marchiori

View down the stairs from restaurant

WESTIN HOTEL TABOR CENTER
Denver, Colorado
Main Ballroom

Typical Guest Room

Photographer: Phillip Nilsson

Suite

Photographer: Dean J. Birinyi

Breakfast Area

EMBASSY SUITES
Denver, Colorado
Atrium

Photographer: Phillip Nilsson

Photographer: Phillip Nilsson

Atrium

Photographer: Phillip Nilsson

LOEWS CORONADO BAY
Coronado, California
*Grand Stair – A 450-room
hotel set on the water's
edge in a very exclusive
residential neighborhood.*

LOEWS CORONADO BAY
Coronado, California
Suite Living Room

IMPERIAL HOTEL
Tokyo, Japan
Eureka Restaurant

BARRY DESIGN ASSOCIATES, INC.

11601 Wilshire Boulevard, Suite 102, Los Angeles, CA 90025
310/478 6081, Fax: 310/312 9926

BARRY DESIGN ASSOCIATES

Barry Design Associates, Inc. provides hoteliers – and their guests – "safe harbor" from the cliches of ordinary hotel and restaurant interior design. ☐ Limited neither by allegiance to a single design style, nor the ever-passing parade of faddishness, Barry Design creates *integrative interior architecture* that is sensitive to the concerns of hoteliers and their guests alike, surrounding architecture and the larger environment. Cognizant of the past as well as the future, budgets as well as location, the firm works closely with owners and operators to bring the myriad elements of successful hospitality design into clear and manageable view. Barry Design also offers a complete Graphic Design Department with considerable experience and expertise in the interior graphic design of hotels. ☐ Projects by Barry Design Associates begin with the timeless ideals of comfort and satisfaction, and end with a sense of place and elegance.

GRAND HYATT WAILEA,
Maui, Hawaii
Spa reception – 50,000 sq. ft. This is truly luxurious in the fashion of the Ritz in Paris. Reception area has a traditional Venetian chandelier and trompe l'oeil ceiling and walls.

GRAND HYATT WAILEA,
Maui, Hawaii
Atrium lobby bar – The ceiling has a mural depicting early Hawaiians.

STOUFFER WAILEA,
Maui, Hawaii
Registration Lobby – A beige
scheme to emphasize the color of
beautiful surrounding grounds.

STOUFFER WAILEA,
Maui, Hawaii
Grand Stair – 300-room
luxury hotel with a
5-star rating for eleven
years – only two other
hotels in Hawaii are
5-star rated.

STOUFFER WAILEA,
Maui, Hawaii
Aloha Suite bath

STOUFFER WAILEA,
Maui, Hawaii
Aloha Suite bedroom

GRAND HYATT WAILEA,
Maui, Hawaii
Ballroom with view of
mural – 28,000 sq. ft.
The chandelier is 60
feet long with each leaf
and flower handmade in
Murano, Italy.

GRAND HYATT WAILEA,
Maui, Hawaii
Formal Restaurant – "The Maui"

HYATT REGENCY LAX
Los Angeles, California

HYATT REGENCY LAX
Los Angeles, California
670-room hotel at the
Los Angeles Airport

RADISSON HOTEL
Tuscon, Arizona
Westwood Grill

RADISSON HOTEL
Tuscon, Arizona
Westwood Grill

NATIONAL RECOGNITION

Interior Design Magazine

Designers West

Commercial Rennovation

Restaurant/Hotel Design International

Professional Builder

Interiors Magazine

Travel Agent

Orange County Magazine

BRASELLE DESIGN COMPANY

423 Thirty-First Street, Newport Beach, California 92663
714/673-6522, Fax: 714/673-2461

BRASELLE DESIGN COMPANY

Braselle Design Company is a full service interior design firm dedicated to innovative design for the commercial and hospitality industry. ▭ Their principal, Meriam Braselle, formed Braselle Design in 1976. Since then, she has produced award-winning interior designs throughout the United States and Canada. Her ability to focus on clients' individual needs and requirements has enabled the firm to establish a repeat client

base with nationally recognized restaurateurs and hoteliers. ▭ Much of the firm's success lies in the detail given to each project. Every client receives Ms. Braselle's individual attention. The firm's focus has consistently been to grow better, not necessarily bigger: A well trained design and administrative support staff executes aesthetic and budgetary criteria smoothly and efficiently. ▭ The firm's goal is to provide each client with the highest quality project possible within the budgetary and time constraints. Keen attention is constantly paid to the bottom line. ▭ Providing professional, innovative design with attention to detail and an unprecedented level of personal service - at Braselle Design Company, it's just good business.

43

SHERATON NEWPORT HOTEL
Newport Beach, California
Palm Court Dining

SHERATON NEWPORT HOTEL
Newport Beach, California
Guestroom

SHERATON NEWPORT HOTEL
Newport Beach, California
Conference Area

SHERATON ANAHEIM HOTEL
Anaheim, California
Lobby

SHERATON ANAHEIM HOTEL
Anaheim, California
Patio at Garden Dining

SHERATON ANAHEIM HOTEL
Anaheim, California
Garden Dining

Photographer: Peter Paige

SHERATON SUITES PLANTATION
Plantation, Florida
*The Plantation Grill features an
exquisite landscape mural
enhancing the plantation theme.*

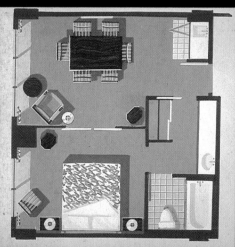

SHERATON SUITES PROTOTYPE
Typical Suite Layout

BRENNAN BEER GORMAN/ARCHITECTS
BRENNAN BEER GORMAN MONK/INTERIORS

515 Madison Avenue
New York, New York, 10022
212/888-7663, Fax: 212/935-3868

1155 21st Street NW
Washington D.C. 20036
202/452-1644, Fax: 202/452-1647

19/F Queen's Place
74 Queens Road, Central Hong Kong
852/525-9766, Fax: 852/525-9850

BRENNAN BEER GORMAN/ARCHITECTS
BRENNAN BEER GORMAN MONK/INTERIORS

Brennan Beer Gorman/Architects and Brennan Beer Gorman Monk/Interiors have a special expertise in ;the architectural and interior design of hospitality projects. The firms were ranked No. 1 in the most recent *Hotel & Motel Managment's* lodging design survey of the top 25 firms in the United States. ☐ The firm's experience in new hotel design provided the foundation for their continuing success with hotel renovation. Working in accordance with physical and budgetary guidelines, the design staff creates unique, efficient and profitable environments for each hotel. Many hospitality design projects function as a city-within-a-city, combining efficient facilities for living, dining, meeting, shopping and recreation. ☐ The founding partners of the firms have over 25 years of hospitality design experience working with national and international operations such as Hilton International, Hyatt, Inter-Continental, ITT Sheraton Corporation, Omni, Ritz-Carlton, Peninsula, Hong Kong

Shanghai Hotel Ltd., and Ramada. Project sites include the United States, New Zealand, Thailand, The Philippines, Malaysia, The People's Republic of China, Iran, Egypt, Zaire and Russia. Brennan Beer Gorman/Architects and Brennan Beer Gorman Monk/Interiors have offices in New York, Washington DC and Hong Kong.

Photographer Peter Paige

SHERATON SUITES PLANTATION
Plantation, Florida
A landscaped courtyard, designed with trellis work, richly textured paving and central fountain is the focal point of both the hotel and the adjacent Plantation Fashion Mall.

SHERATON SUITES PLANTATION
Plantation, Florida
Rooftop swimming pool and health club feature sweeping views of the Fort Lauderdale and Plantation area.

Photographer Peter Paige

SHERRY NETHERLAND
New York, New York
Living Room
Elegant furnishings reflect 18th century styling and feature richly patterned fabrics in damasds, stripes and solids.

Photographer: Daniel Aubrey

SHERRY NETHERLAND
New York, New York
Double Bedroom
Rich fabrics in deep blues and golds highlight the grand scale in this inviting double bedroom.

Photographer: Daniel Aubrey

Photographer: Daniel Aubrey

SHERRY NETHERLAND
New York, New York
King Bedroom
The graciously scaled king bedroom with luxurious fabrics offers a warm residential ambiance that appeals to extended stay guests as well as frequent business and leisure travelers.

COURTYARD BY MARRIOTT
Washington, DC
The Presidential Suite employs a rich jewel tone color palatte, highlighted with touches of gold.

COURTYARD BY MARRIOTT
Washington, DC
The hotel's lobby is framed by mahogany-clad columns and elegantly accented by Waterford crystal chandeliers.

COURTYARD BY MARRIOTT
Washington, DC
The Presidential Suite bathroom is designed with a verde marble vanity top juxtaposed with crema mardil marble to create a gracious and spacious effect.

QUALITY HOTEL CENTRAL
Washington, DC
Claret's, a full service restaurant that doubles as a function room, was conceived as a light and airy room, with a terrace theme.

49

KEA LANI HOTEL
Wailea, Maui, Hawaii
*Guest room corridor/elevator
lobby at dusk*

COLE MARTINEZ CURTIS AND ASSOCIATES

308 Washington Boulevard, Marina del Rey, California 90292
310/827-7200, Fax: 310/822-5803

COLE MARTINEZ CURTIS AND ASSOCIATES

Cole Martinez Curtis and Associates recently celebrated a quarter century of creating interior spaces for an international clientele. From its modest beginnings in 1967, the firm has grown to its current size of 70 who staff the Marina del Rey, California headquarters. Under the direction of principals Jill Cole and Leo Martinez, the full-service firm has diversified to include expertise in all phases of hospitality, retail store, and commercial design as well as furniture purchasing and expediting.

Over the years, Cole Martinez Curtis and Associates has been dedicated to providing quality service and design that is responsive to the client's needs and image. The firm's commitment to these standards has resulted in several award-winning projects including The Adolphus Hotel, Dallas, Texas; The Newporter Resort, Newport Beach, California; and The Wigwam Resort, Litchfield Park, Arizona. The firm's recent hospitality work includes the Hilton Head Island Hilton Resort; Marriott Ownership Resort, Park City, Utah; and the Starr Pass Clubhouse and Villas, Tucson, Arizona.

KEA LANI HOTEL
Wailea, Maui, Hawaii
Registration Lobby
The hotel's European-influenced interior is unique to the resort's Hawaiian setting and a contrast to its Moorish architecture.

Lobby Lounge
The gentle arches of the custom-designed railing hint at the Moorish architecture. The handmade carpet was also custom-designed.

Floor plan of Kea Lani Restaurant.

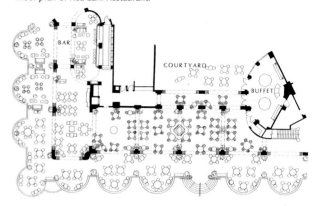

The Kea Lani Restaurant's immense space is visually divided into two areas, one formal and the other casual, and features custom-designed, pineapple backed wood-frame chairs.

Boardroom

The Kea Lani Restaurant
The casual dining area in the Kea Lani Restaurant is furnished with custom-designed, metal garden-style chairs with tie-on cushions.

Floor plan of Registration Lobby and Lobby Lounge.

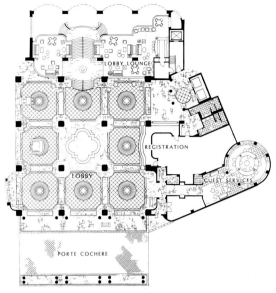

Floor plan of typical suite.

Guest Room Corridor/Elevator Lobby
A rattan seating group, located in the elevator lobbies on each floor of the hotel, invites guests to linger and enjoy the view.

Guest Room Living Room
Each suite was planned to have a living room, bedroom, bath, mini-kitchen, and private lanai in Maui's only all-suite hotel.

The European-style, marble guest suite bathrooms were purposely oversized and feature a large soaking tub, separate shower, and two basins.

HILTON WATERFRONT
Huntington Beach, California
Upper Lobby Lounge

HILTON WATERFRONT
Huntington Beach, California
Lower Lobby Lounge

CONCEPTS 4, INC.

300 North Continental, Suite 320, El Segundo, California 90245
310/640-0290, Fax: 310/640-0009

CONCEPTS 4, INC.

Concepts 4, Inc., established in 1977, is a firm of experts in management and design whose comprehension of the hospitality industry enables them to create hotels of both distinctive design and unparalleled edge for profitability.

Architecture, interior design, construction, and management are the four essential elements in a successful hotel operation; the interaction of these disciplines is the underlying principle of the firm. Founders Jerry Howard, John Mamer, and Dennis Darlington have been specialists in the hospitality industry for more than 20 years. As former hotel owners themselves, they tailor their formula to each client, insuring a product that is as visually exciting as it is functional.

SHERATON SCOTTSDALE
Scottsdale, Arizona
Remington's Restaurant

SHERATON SCOTTSDALE
Scottsdale, Arizona
Presidential Suite

SHERATON SCOTTSDALE
Scottsdale, Arizona
Entry Foyer to Remington's

SHERATON SCOTTSDALE
Scottsdale, Arizona
Vice Presidential Suite

SHERATON SCOTTSDALE
Scottsdale, Arizona
Lobby Bar

WESTIN MISSION HILLS RESORT
Rancho Mirage, California
Presidential Suite
Living Room

WESTIN MISSION HILLS RESORT
Rancho Mirage, California
Chairman's Suite
Bedroom

WESTIN MISSION HILLS RESORT
Rancho Mirage, California
Chairman's Suite
Living Room

57

DISNEY'S DIXIE LANDINGS RESORT
Lake Buena Vista, Florida

The steamship depot theme is articulated in the registration area complete with working "punkah" ceiling fans, trunks and "ticket agent" windows at the registration desk.

The merchandise area of this resort is housed in Fulton's General Store.

DAROFF DESIGN INC

2300 Ionic Street, Philadelphia, PA 19103
215/636-9900, Fax: 215/636-9627

DAROFF DESIGN INC

Daroff Design Inc. (a certified Woman's Business Enterprise) and its affiliate companies, DDI Architects, P.C. and DDI Graphics, provide comprehensive interior architectural and graphic design services for the hospitality industry. ⊏⊐ The firm, founded in 1973 by Karen Daroff, currently employs 40 professionals who are skilled in producing innovative yet highly functional and cost-effective interiors for conference and training, destination and gaming resorts and facilities catering to the business traveler. ⊏⊐ Daroff Design Inc. has an impressive portfolio of award-winning projects representing many diverse design styles from thematic to traditional and wide range of budgets, from modest to five-star luxury accommodations, for renovation and new construction projects.

⊏⊐ The firm's recent highly acclaimed projects include The Sagamore Hotel and Conference Center, Disney's Contemp-orary Resort Hotel (recipient of the Orlando AIA Chapter 1993 award for design excellence), Disney's Dixie Landings Resort, Scanticon Hotel and Conference Center, Philadelphia Marriott Convention Center Hotel, Great Valley Hilton and Conference Center, several casino properties and the newly renovated Philadelphia Embassy Suites Hotel.

DISNEY'S DIXIE LANDINGS RESORT
Lake Buena Vista, Florida
Fugleberg Koch Architects, Inc./Architect
Daroff Design Inc/Interior
Architectural Design

As guests enter the lobby, they are reminded of a steamship company headquarters of a bygone era. It features an unusual custom-designed wood floor in a compass pattern.

DISNEY'S DIXIE LANDINGS RESORT
Lake Buena Vista, Florida

The full-service, sit-down restaurant has been designed to be reminiscent of a 19th century Boatwright shop. The elevated exposed skeleton of a boat in construction captures the spirit.

The boatwright dining area incorporates actual woodworking tools as wall decor and an eclectic assortment of wooden chairs and rustic furnishings.

Photographer: Elliott Kaufman

The food court servery has been designed as a festive farmer's market, complete with colorful awnings, tile flooring in a cobblestone design and distinctly identifiable "shopfronts."

Photographer: Elliott Kaufman

The casual food court dining area represents a cavernous cotton mill, with bales of fresh harvest, a massive working waterwheel and a giant cotton press.

Photographer: Elliott Kaufman

**DISNEY'S CONTEMPORARY
RESORT HOTEL**
Lake Buena Vista, Florida
DDI Architects, P.C./
Architect of Record
Daroff Design Inc/Interior
Architectural, Graphics
and Signage Design

The lobby, originally designed in the early 1970s, was renovated in a highly contemporary thematic design spirit. Floating ceiling planes, cove lighting and marble floors enhance the drama and excitement of this space.

Photographer: Elliott Kaufman

The lobby seating area features contemporary furnishings in vibrant accent colors that accentuate the unusual curves and lines of the space.

Photographer: Elliott Kaufman

The Tamo Ash custom millwork registration counter has been designed to facilitate large group check-ins.

Photographer: Elliott Kaufman

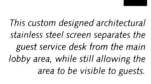

This custom designed architectural stainless steel screen separates the guest service desk from the main lobby area, while still allowing the area to be visible to guests.

Photographer: Elliott Kaufman

Photographer: Paul Warchol

**THE SAGAMORE HOTEL
AND CONFERENCE CENTER
Bolton's Landing
Lake George, New York
Alesker Reiff & Dundon/Architect
Daroff Design Inc/Interior
Architectural Design, Graphics,
Signage, Table Top and Uniforms**

*The Sagamore Hotel was originally
opened as a private vacation resort in
1883 for five prominent Philadelphia
families. This historically-certified
structure was restored, expanded
and re-opened as a 350-room
Omni Classic Hotel.*

*The glass enclosed veranda/piano
lounge with its beautiful white pillars
is operational year-round and affords
a beautiful view of scenic Lake George.*

Photographer: Paul Warchol

reception/arrival building ated ro reduce congestion in the hotel's main lobby.

The Trillium Restaurant's historic architectural detailing was carefully preserved and incorporated into the design of this elegant, full-service dining room.

BIGHORN COUNTRY CLUB
Palm Desert, California
Gallery

Clients:

Disney Development
 Corporation
Mark IV Properties
Ken International
Westinghouse Desert
 Communities
Hong Kong Country Club
 Association

BIGHORN COUNTRY CLUB
Palm Desert, California
Lobby

DESIGN 1 INTERIORS

LOS ANGELES   PARIS   HONG KONG

2049 Century Park East, Suite 3000, Los Angeles, California 90067
310 553-5032, Fax: 310 785-0445

DESIGN 1 INTERIORS

Design 1 Interiors is a full-service organization dedicated to producing exceptional interior designs for the hospitality and club industries, restaurants and residential developments. ▭ The firm's steady growth and success can be attributed to its solid business management and astute sense of using interior design as a means to merchandise a product. ▭ Each of Design 1's projects is developed individually with careful attention paid to specific market trends and client needs. Designs are targeted toward a particular market as well as the project's overall theme in order to achieve the client's desired objective: to profitably and efficiently operate a property. ▭ Design 1 Interiors is not associated with a single "look"; instead they combine an array of tastes with all the elements of a property to form the perfect environment. Coupled with the constant search for the finest artisans with the most competitive prices, Design 1's clients can be assured that every space functions effectively as well as aesthetically. ▭ Design 1 Interiors has earned its international reputation for creatively producing timeless designs on schedule and within budget.

DISNEY'S VACATION CLUB RESORT
Orlando, Florida
"Papa's Den" Guest Lounge ('a la Hemingway)

PALA MESA RESORT
Fallbrook, California
Registration Lobby
(Renovation)

Photographer: Robb Miller

Photographer: Robb Miller

PALA MESA RESORT
Fallbrook, California
Typical Guestroom
(Renovation)

Photographer: Kerun IP

HONG KONG COUNTRY CLUB
Deep Water Bay, Hong Kong
Grill Room
(Renovation)

HOTEL INDIAN WELLS
Indian Wells, California
Public Restroom Facility
(Renovation)

HOTEL INDIAN WELLS
Indian Wells, California
Presidential Suite Bedroom
(Renovation)

Photographer: Martin Fine

Photographer: Milroy/McAleer

HOTEL INDIAN WELLS
Indian Wells, California
Reception Lobby
(Renovation)

Photographer: Martin Fine

69

GROVE PARK INN
Asheville, North Carolina
*Much of the original Roycrofters' furniture and
lighting was kept for the restoration of this hotel.*

Other Projects:

The Breakers
Palm Beach, Florida

Marriott's Bay Point Resort
Panama City, Florida

Marriott's Cypress Harbour Resort
Orlando, Florida

Newport Bay Club Hotel, Euro Disney
Paris, France

Embassy Suites Hotels in Chicago,
Orlando, San Diego and Washington, DC

DESIGN CONTINUUM, INC.

Five Piedmont Center, Suite 300, Atlanta, Georgia 30305
404/266-0095, Fax: 404/266-8252

DESIGN CONTINUUM, INC.

Atlanta-based Design Continuum specializes in the design of hotels, restaurants, private city clubs and country clubs. Their twenty-one years of hospitality design experience and careful attention to detail enable them to provide highly successful interiors for urban hotels, convention/conference properties and major destination resorts throughout the United States, Canada, Europe and Japan. The firm's designs for resort properties

have been nationally recognized for their own distinct and individual characteristics. ☐ In addition to their creativity and enthusiasm, the firm's commitment to providing excellent personal service has resulted in a prominent reputation and a continuing and ever increasing list of repeat clients. ☐ The staff's varied architectural and interior design backgrounds create competence in a variety of design styles including historic restorations, adaptive reuse, transitional, eclectic and contemporary idioms. The high quality and accuracy of their working drawings and furnishing specifications enable them to plan and design with pre-agreed budgetary constraints and accelerated time frames.

J. W. MARRIOTT
Atlanta, Georgia
Traditional southern ambiance in the lobby of this hotel in Atlanta's upscale Buckhead area.

Photographed Ira Montgomery

71

DISNEY'S YACHT CLUB RESORT
Orlando, Florida
The Convention Center gallery leads to the grand ballroom and individual conference rooms.

Disney's Convention Center Floor Plan

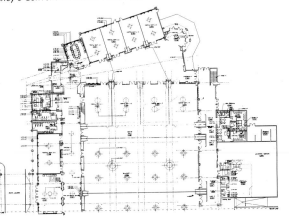

Photographer: Robert Miller

DON CE SAR
St. Petersburg, Florida
This renovation made the hotel lighter, brighter and more opulent than ever.

Photographer: Milroy McAleer

Photographer: Robert Miller

DISNEY'S YACHT CLUB RESORT
Orlando, Florida
The double height Yacht Club lobby has the gracious quality of a New England turn-of-the-century club.

Fairmount Third Floor Plan

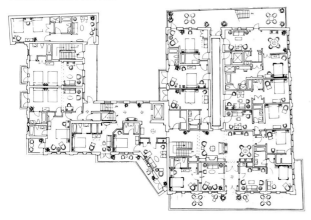

INTER-CONTINENTAL
Chicago, Illinois
The lavish Renaissance Room features richly paneled walls of Carpathian elm burlwood.

Photographer: Ira Montgomery

FAIRMOUNT
San Antonio, Texas
The scale is intimate and personal in a typical guest suite.

Photographer: Ira Montgomery

INTER-CONTINENTAL
Los Angeles, California
The light colors and soft, inviting seating with loose pillows create a "California casual" feeling.

Photographer: Milroy McAleer

THE ROYAL ABJAR HOTEL
Dubai, United Arab Emirates
Oasis Lounge Bar

The Royal Abjar Hotel - Lobby Level

The Royal Abjar Hotel - Lobby Level

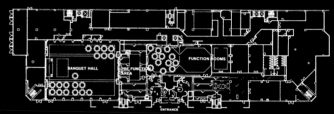

GROUND FLOOR LEVEL

Main Lobby
The use of water, plants cascading
from bridges, and cool fabric colors
suggests an "oasis" feeling.

DI LEONARDO INTERNATIONAL, INC.

2350 Post Road, Suite 1
Warwick, Rhode Island 02886-2242
401/732-2900, Fax. 401/732-5315

The Centre Mark Building, Room 608
287-289 Queen's Road, Central, Hong Kong
852/851-7282, 851-7227, Fax. 852/851-7287

DI LEONARDO INTERNATIONAL, INC.

Di Leonardo International, Inc. has established itself as one of the most prominent hospitality interior design firms in the world through the quality of its work and through its consistently outstanding level of service. In addition to hotels, they design golf club houses, casinos, conference centers, cruise ships, and restaurants. ☐ The firm ensures a smooth transition from a project's conceptual stage through its successful completion by offering schematic design, design development, construction documentation, budget control and project administration. By carefully controlling and administering each stage of a project, they are able to provide their clients with problem free and exceptional service. ☐ Di Leonardo International's full range of interior design capabilities include graphic, lighting and acoustical designs, furnishing specification, and art/accessory selection and purchasing; and menu and kitchen design. ☐ Through their 20 years of designing worldwide for clients in the hospitality industry, they have learned to design profitable facilities exceptionally well and have attained an unmatched level of excellence.

THE ROYAL ABJAR HOTEL
Dubai, United Arab Emirates
Grand Ballroom

Camel Coffee Shop

THE NEW WORLD HOTEL
Kowloon, Hong Kong
Main Lobby
The overall concept was to create something that is timeless in design and add a whole new dimension to what a contemporary experience would be.

New World Hotel Hong Kong - Floor Plan

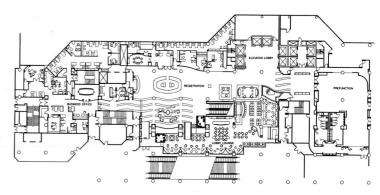

Main Lobby

Registration Desk
Some "fun" was created in the design, yet at a level where it maintained a high degree of sophistication.

THE NEW WORLD HOTEL
Kowloon, Hong Kong
Main Lobby
The overall concept was to create something that is timeless in design and add a whole new dimension to what a contemporary experience would be.

THE RENAISSANCE HOTEL
Times Square, New York City
Elevator Lobby
The interior throughout is clad in a harmonious background of highly figured wood and lustrous finishes, creating a sleek "club-like" atmosphere for this hotel's relatively small-scale footprint.

Guest Bedroom

Main Dining Room
The use of luxurious materials and subtle color combinations produces a sophisticated setting.

Photographer: Dan Forer

Reception Lobby - Registration Area

Photographer: Dan Forer

DIANNE JOYCE DESIGN GROUP, INC.

The Dianne Joyce Design Group, Inc. is a full service contract interior design firm. Formed in 1978, their work has achieved national recognition through numerous publications and awards. Adept at planning and designing new construction and renovations, the staff has completed a wide variety of projects ranging from hotels, restaurants, corporate complexes and international banking facilities, to residences of extraordinary character. ▭ A full complement of interior architects, designers, draftsmen, production and support personnel share a common design language and dedication to excellence. This has allowed the firm to build a solid base of ongoing work for clients such as Disney Development, Prudential, Sandals Resorts, Codina Bush Group, Hyatt Corporation and other prestigious groups. ▭ Believing in a team approach, they have combined the talents of their designers with the finest contractors and consultants to secure the best efforts of the team.

DISNEY'S PORT ORLEANS RESORT
Disney World, Orlando, Florida
Mardi Gras Food Court designed to duplicate the staging area in which the mardi gras floats are assembled.

Photographer: Dan Forer

79

Photographer: Dan Forer

HOTEL NIKKO
Atlanta, Georgia
Chassis Restaurant
Overall view of the hotel's more formal dining room, which was designed with a French flair.

Photographer: Dan Forer

Photographer: Dan Forer

Detail of lobby lounge with Japanese garden beyond

Detail of Presidential Suite, dining room

Elevator Cab

Photographer: Dan Forer

Nikko Lounge
Sits at the top of the hotel and serves as an extra support area for concierge level customers.

Photographer: Dan Forer

Library Bar

Photographer: Dan Forer

EVERETT HOLIDAY INN
Everett, Washington
Lobby (renovation)

DOW/FLETCHER

127 Bellevue Way SE, Suite 100, Bellevue, Washington 98004
206/454-0029, Fax: 206/646-5904

DOW/FLETCHER

Dow/Fletcher is in its 12th year of service to the hospitality industry. They are unique because the principals of the firm are experienced in managing hotels and approach each project with a special understanding of developers needs. Besides providing architectural, interior design and furniture, fixtures and equipment purchasing services, They offer general contracting/construction management. They feel the best possible method of accomplishing projects from an owner's standpoint is "Design/Build"—the development and implementation of design solutions. Tremendous financial advantages and completion efficiencies are the result of this program which is particularly apparent in renovations. With associate offices in London and Taipei, they are truly a global design and purchasing company with the bonus of real construction and hotel operations savvy.

EDGEWATER HOTEL
Seattle, Washington
Lobby of downtown waterfront hotel (renovation)

PORTOFINO INN AT THE MARINA
Redondo Beach, California
Lobby (renovation)

■ **SEATTLE RAMADA HOTEL**
Seattle, Washington
Lobby of downtown
hotel (renovation)

■ **WEST COAST INTERNATIONAL INN**
Anchorage, Alaska
Lobby (renovation)

BEST WESTERN ICICLE INN
Leavenworth, Washington
Guestroom

WEST COAST WENATCHEE
CENTER HOTEL
Wenatchee, WA
Lobby (renovation)

BEST WESTERN ICICLE INN
Leavenworth, Washington
Lobby

PARADISE BEACH HOTEL
Pusan, South Korea
Japanese Restaurant

HAROLD THOMPSON & ASSOCIATES

15260 Ventura Boulevard, Suite 1910, Sherman Oaks, California 91403
818/789-3005, Fax: 818/789-3089

HAROLD THOMPSON & ASSOCIATES

Over a period of ten years, Harold Thompson & Associates has proudly developed a dedicated team of professionals who have become adept at solving design problems, individually and collectively. The firm is a totally self-contained group of professionals including an Art and Graphics Staff that handles special problems. ⊏⊐ Although versed in all aspects of interior design, Harold Thompson & Associates specializes in hotels, with particular attention to the challenges presented. They understand that a hotel is a complex plant, requiring multi-faceted talents from functional planning to aesthetic and artistic evironment. ⊏⊐ Through a continuous learning curve, a vast amount of knowledge in putting together these complex projects has been accumulated under one roof. Harold Thompson & Associates understand the needs, timing, economics, merchandising, aesthetics and practical operation of a hotel. ⊏⊐ They are artists, but do not live in a vacuum, believing communication is necessary for success. They are proud to have completed many fine projects for clients who have continued to request their services.

PARADISE BEACH HOTEL
Pusan, South Korea
Lobby Lounge

PARADISE BEACH HOTEL
Pusan, South Korea
Korean Style Suite

PARADISE BEACH HOTEL
Pusan, South Korea
Guestroom

PARADISE BEACH HOTEL
Pusan, South Korea
2 Bay Suite

PARADISE BEACH HOTEL
Pusan, South Korea
Casino Stair

PARADISE BEACH HOTEL
Pusan, South Korea
Japanese Restaurant

PARADISE BEACH HOTEL
Pusan, South Korea
Korean Restaurant

MELBOURNE, AUSTRALIA
*Luxurious marble
corridor of urban hotel*

BELGRADE, YUGOSLAVIA
*Intimate dining area
in elegant hotel*

HIRSCH/BEDNER ASSOCIATES

3216 Nebraska Avenue
Santa Monica, California 90404
310/829-9087, Fax 310/453-1182

49 Wellington Street
London, England WC2E 7BN
071/240-2099, Fax 071/240-2050

4/F Kai Tak Commercial Building
317-321 Des Voeux Road
Central Hong Kong
852/542-2022, Fax 852/545-2051

11 Stamford Road
#02-08 Capitol Building
Singapore 0617
65-337-2511, Fax 65-337-2460

909 W. Peachtree Street, N.E.
Atlanta, Georgia
404/873-4379, Fax 404/872-3588

HIRSCH/BEDNER ASSOCIATES

With 340 projects completed worldwide during the past twenty-seven years, Hirsch/Bedner Associates has explored and developed every aspect of diverse hotel design ranging from twenty-room "boutique" hotels to two-thousand room convention hotels. This international group of professional hotel designers offers their expertise to each stage on every project with a researched understanding of its geographical, cultural, operational and financial characteristics. This special approach creates the design excellence for which H/BA has been widely recognized. ☐ The company's success can be attributed to the superior standards established for each project with close attention given to every phase and detail, and with the addition of specialized individual services of purchasing, art procurement and graphics.

DEAUVILLE, FRANCE
Gaming room from historic renovation

HONG KONG
Grand lobby of 575-room contemporary hotel

CHICAGO, ILLINOIS
*Entrance to grand ballroom
of historic hotel*

MONTEREY, CALIFORNIA
*Comfortable lobby/lounge
of resort and clubhouse*

**ARUBA,
CARIBBEAN ISLANDS**
*Open air lobby of
390-room resort hotel*

━ **OKINAWA, JAPAN**
*Atrium lobby of
private clubhouse*

▌ **MAUI, HAWAII**
*Open air dining area surrounded
by waterfalls and tropical birds*

━ **SAN FRANCISCO, CALIFORNIA**
*Unique design of guestroom for
hotel at Embarcadero Center*

THE RICHMOND AIRPORT HILTON
Richmond, Virginia

Lobby
The entrance seating group exhibits a contemporary Frank Lloyd Wright flavor which the designer incorporated into the interiors to reflect the architect's treatment of the building's exterior.

THE SHERATON MANHATTAN HOTEL
New York, New York

Bistro 790
Not one downlight mars the hand painted ceiling vault. Indirect lighting is provided by miniature sources concealed in slim, floating beams which reflect off the colorful ceiling.

Photographer: Peter Paige

THE RICHMOND AIRPORT HILTON
Richmond, Virginia

Corridor
Public corridors provide continuity to the Frank Lloyd Wright influence experienced upon entering the hotel.

Photographer: Peter Paige

HOCHHEISER ELIAS DESIGN GROUP, INC.

226 East 54th Street, New York, New York 10022
212/826-8700, Fax: 212/826-8703

HOCHHEISER-ELIAS DESIGN GROUP, INC.

Hochheiser-Elias design group inc. practices hospitality design according to its philosophy of "Performance Design." To meet the H-Elias criteria for performance design, each solution must be aesthetically exciting and must fulfill the expectations of the target market. It must also make economic sense for the client in terms of the initial investment, the longevity of aesthetics and the durability of the materials, construction details and finishes. ☐ The firm has received virtually every industry design award; and with a very large design vocabulary, has completed projects ranging from historic preservation to "cutting edge," new wave. ☐ Equally important to the firm's design capabilities is the execution of the design. H-Elias is cited for providing the best detail and documentation package in the industry; for meeting budget goals and for on time performance. ☐ Current projects include the Sheraton New York, The Sheraton Manhattan, The Waldorf Astoria, The Fountainbleau, The Sheraton Washington, The Hilton at Disney World and The New York Hilton.

**THE JEFFERSON HOTEL
RICHMOND, VIRGINIA**
Signature Restaurant
Recessed low voltage lighting, hand woven rugs, and contemporary etched glass are blended with the architectural elements in this historically certified property to create a dramatic introduction to this fine dining experience.

Photographer: Whitney Cox

**THE JEFFERSON HOTEL
RICHMOND, VIRGINIA**
The Atrium
This historically certified property was restored to its original grandeur with marbleized columns finished in the old scagiola method. The Grand Stair served as the model for Tara in "Gone with the Wind."

Photographer: Whitney Cox

THE SHERATON CARLTON
Washington, DC
Lobby
The lobby of this historic hotel has been sensitively restored. Period furnishings are rendered in a contemporary palette and concealed state-of-the-art lighting emphasizes the detailed ceiling and highlights the antique chandeliers.

THE SHERATON CARLTON
Washington, DC
Presidential Suite Bedroom
This elegant, award-winning bedroom, belies its security systems complete with bullet proof glass and adjacent guard facilities required by its location near the Capitol.

Photographer: Peter Paige

Photographer: Peter Paige

THE SHERATON CARLTON
Washington, DC
Presidential Suite Dining Room
Document wallcovering and reproduction American 1800's period furniture reflect the hotel's location two blocks from the nation's Capitol building.

Photographer: Peter Paige

THE SHERATON CARLTON
Washington, DC
Allegro Restaurant
Indirect lighting reflected off the 100-year-old hand painted ceiling creates the ambiance of a sunset in Rome. The Washington Post cites this room as one of the most romantic in the nation's capital.

THE SHERATON CARLTON
Washington, DC
Guestroom
Furnishings were custom designed for these luxury guestrooms which were awarded the Gold Key for Excellence in design by the American Hotel and Motel Association.

Photographer: Peter Paige

THE SHERATON WASHINGTON
Washington, DC
Americus Restaurant
Situated on the atrium balcony at this convention hotel, the restaurant provides a "see and be seen atmosphere" for guests. The sparkle and glamour enliven the entire lobby.

Photographer: Peter Paige

COLONNADE HOTEL
Coral Gables, Florida

HOWARD LUACES & ASSOCIATES

5785 Sunset Drive, South Miami, Florida 33143
305 662-9002, Fax 305 662-7006

HOWARD-LUACES & ASSOCIATES

Howard-Luaces & Associates is a commercial interior design firm specializing in space planning. The firm has completed such projects as Turnberry Isle Hotel and Country Club, The Colonnade Hotel (Coral Gables), the Mayfair House Hotel, The Ponahawaii Clubhouse (Hilo, Hawaii) and Condado Beach Hotel & Casino (Puerto Rico). ☐ They have been commissioned to design hotels for such major corporations as The Continental Companies, Prudential Insurance Company of America, Aetna Life & Casualty, Equitable Life Insurance Company, Radice Corporation, Intercap Investments, Inc., and Tishman/CP Hotels. The firm's work has received national recognition in such magazines as *Contract, Interior Design, Florida Designers Quarterly* and *Lodging Hospitality*. Their work has also received the IBD National Competition Award, the Shelby Williams Silver Anniversary Contract Award, and the highly acclaimed Gold Key Award. ☐ With their expertise in interior design, Howard-Luaces & Associates can provide complete contractual design services to include presentation, computer aided design drawings, renderings both interior and exterior, specifications and purchasing.

WESTIN
Fort Lauderdale, Florida

GRAND BAY
New York, New York

TURNBERRY ISLE HOTEL
Miami, Florida

GRAND BAY
Coconut Grove, Florida

■ HYATT
Coral Gables, Florida

■ HYATT
Coral Gables, Florida

■ WILLIAMS ISLAND
Miami, Florida

SHANGHAI CENTRE
Shanghai, China
Lobby Staircase

SHANGHAI CENTRE
Shanghai, China
Exterior Architecture

SHANGHAI CENTRE
Shanghai, China
Atrium Lobby

JOHN PORTMAN & ASSOCIATES

John Portman & Associates, the flagship of The Portman Companies, provides distinctive architectural, engineering and interior design services on projects ranging from hotels and mixed-use urban complexes to individual commercial and institutional buildings. The impact of the firm's work on the hospitality industry has been dramatic. Portman's first hotel in 1967, the Hyatt Regency Atlanta, revolutionized hotel design with the introduction of the modern atrium. The architectural interior of the hotel awoke new design possibilities. ☐ Subsequent work earned the American Institute of Architects Medal for Innovations in Hotel Design and the Elsie deWolfe Award from the American Institute of Interior Designers. ☐ Hotels designed by the firm include: Atlanta Marriott Marquis and the Westin Peachtree Plaza in Atlanta; New York Marriott Marquis in Times Square; Hyatt Regency O'Hare in Chicago, the Hyatt Regency and the Park Hyatt at Embarcadero Center in San Francisco; and the Pan Pacific, Oriental, Madarin and Regent hotels—all in Singapore. Established in Atlanta in 1953, the firm has branch offices in Shanghai and Hong Kong.

THE PAN PACIFIC SAN FRANCISCO
San Francisco, California
The miniature lights add sparkle throughout the lobby and are incorporated in the sculptural chandelier in the elevator lobby.

Photographer Jaime Ardiles-Arce

The atrium lobby focuses on Joie de Danse, a bronze sculpture by Elbert Weinberg. The arched portal to the elevator lobby echoes the shape of the exterior windows.

Photographer: Jaime Ardiles-Arce

The curved and arched forms of the architecture are redefined in the arched canopy over the registration desk and the elevator forms, both of which are outlined in miniature lights.

The dining room in the Executive Conference Center uses polished black wooden chairs and service bar to accent the rich tones of marble, wood and linen.

Photographer: Jaime Ardiles-Arce

Photographer: Jaime Ardiles-Arce

The understated elegance of the lobby bar reinforces the residential quality of the hotel.

Photographer: Jaime Ardiles-Arce

Two fireplaces on the lobby level provide an intimate setting within the atrium giving the space a warm residential quality.

Guest bathrooms were detailed to
include customize-design lighting,
beveled mirrors and Portuguese
marble walls and floors.

■ The master bedroom in the Presidential
Suite is tailored and elegant with
emphasis on a residential quality.

■ A palette of rich material and color
provides an informal yet elegant
sanctuary for guests in The Club
on the 21st floor.

■ The double-sided fireplace
separates the living and dining
areas in the Presidential Suite.

WOODMARK HOTEL
Kirkland, Washington
*The lounge, located at the foot of
stairs, is a vital hub for function
rooms and restaurant.*

WOODMARK HOTEL
Kirkland, Washington
*Lobby
Welcoming and warm,
yet clean and spare*

JOSZI MESKAN ASSOCIATES
INTERIOR ARCHITECTURE AND DESIGN

479 Ninth Street, San Francisco, California 94103
415/431-0500, Fax: 415/431-9339

JOSZI MESKAN ASSOCIATES

People respond to environments without an expert defining exactly what has been done to create them. If the environment is created to entice a customer to buy, then it is truly successful if the customer buys. ▭ The good designer needs only to listen and understand the objectives. The spirit of an interior space connects with a person on a sensual level. Yes, it must be useful, appropriate, efficient, maintainable and cost effective, but yet, it must appeal to the human senses. ▭ Joszi Meskan is principal of a

small atelier firm in San Francisco which has won an international reputation. For 22 years she has been accepting challenges from hotel and ship owners who believe that to take a risk, confidently departing from the crowd, will bring greater success. ▭ That spirit is the inspiration for interiors which have been described as exotic or extravagant or opulent, yet always warm and uniquely personal.

WOODMARK HOTEL
Kirkland, Washington
Lobby Stair
Provides a simple, clean and
spare yet warm atmosphere.

Photographer: Mary Nichols

■ **HARBOR COURT HOTEL**
Baltimore, Maryland
Explorer's Lounge
*In a very relaxed space one can
take high tea with a view toward
the national aquarium.*

■ **HARBOR COURT HOTEL**
Baltimore, Maryland
"Brighton"
*Breakfast Room was designed to
give a feeling as fresh as flowers.*

Photographer: Mary Nichols

Photographer: Mary Nichols

LODGE AT KOELE
Lanai, Hawaii
Library
Island spirit is expressed through hands of local artisans in this exclusive, cool, highland resort. The training of the artisans formed a unique collaboration of local culture and customs in a commercial venture.

Photographer: Mary Nichols

Photographer: Mary Nichols

LODGE AT KOELE
Lanai, Hawaii
Music Room Lounge
A rare collection of instruments adds interest. The hand painted ceiling was inspired by native plants unique only to Lanai.

LODGE AT KOELE
Lanai, Hawaii
Typical Guest Room
Furnishings inspired by antique Phillipine country style with local quilts and pictures. The chairs and end tables are from Thailand and China.

LYNN WILSON
ASSOCIATES INTERNATIONAL

Lynn Wilson Associates International has practiced exclusively in the field of hospitality and hotel design for over 20 years. Working with the major hoteliers, they have been responsible for not only historical restorations and conference hotels but a multitude of luxury resort properties throughout the world. ▭ They have been listed by Hotel Design International and Interior Design magazines as one of the top 10 International Hotel Design Giants consecutively for the past ten years. ▭ Design and production offices are based in Miami, with additional offices in Los Angeles, Paris, Mexico City, Tokyo, Hong Kong and Korea to serve projects over the entire world with a dedicated combined staff of uniquely qualified architects and designers. ▭ Their time-tested disciplines include development of every facet, from conceptual design and space planning to interior architectural drawings and specifications. Their skills are suplemented by state of the art computer systems including CAD, computer specifications, budget and custom control systems that assure aesthetic quality within predetermined budget parameters. ▭ Lynn Wilson's personal integrity and dedication as well as the firm's pride in their work, set Lynn Wilson Associates International's performance for any project as the most talented and valuable asset to the client's professional team.

HOTEL DUPONT
Wilmington, Delaware
Lobby

Floor plan

HOTEL DUPONT
Wilmington, Delaware
Typical Guest Room
Personal Business Center with Fax/Computer

Room Detailing

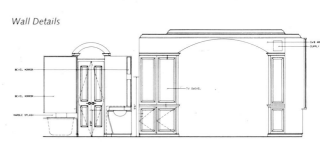

Wall Details

Typical Guest Room Parlour

Luxury Bathroom
For Standard Guest Room

PORT DE PLAISANCE
St. Maarten, Netherlands Antilles

HYATT
Key West, Florida

PORT DE PLAISANCE
St. Maarten, Netherlands Antilles

Coffee Shop

"Diana Sweets" Dining Room

MDI INTERNATIONAL INC.
DESIGN CONSULTANTS

4 Wellington Street East
Fourth Floor
Toronto, Ontario, Canada
M5E 1C5
416/369-0123, Fax: 416/369-0998

Europe/Middle East
74A Kensington Park Road
London, England W11 2LP
4471 727-5683, Fax: 4471 229-2314

Asia/Pacific Rim
11-15 Wing Wo Street Room 501
Wo Hing Commercial Building
Central Hong Kong
852/815-2325, Fax: 852/544-5412

Caribbean/South America
3 Frederick Street, Port of Spain
Trinidad W.I.
809/624-4430, Fax: 809/623-1217

MDI INTERNATIONAL INC.

MDI International Inc., is a full service planning, architectural and interior design firm specializing in the hospitality entertainment, health clubs and restaurant industries. Its founder, Michel Dorais has been designing hotels, restaurants and commercial properties for more than 20 years. ▭ This multilingual firm provides comprehensive design solutions based on its technical expertise and thorough understanding of hotel operations and marketing. Services include feasibility analysis of site and budget, conceptual planning and development leading to the delivery of all design and specification documentation, rendering and supervision of project implementation. ▭ MDI is consistently listed as one of the Hotel Giants in *Interior Design* magazine and as one of the top 50 firms by *Hotel & Management* magazine. ▭ To better service the firm's clientele, MDI maintains offices in Hong Kong, London and Trinidad, and each location offers clients the full range of design services.

Exterior

SHERATON FALLSVIEW
Niagara Falls, Canada
"Joe Bird" Lounge

Corner Suite Wirlpool

Luxury Corner Suite

Main Lobby

Floor Plan 1 - First Floor

Floor Plan 2

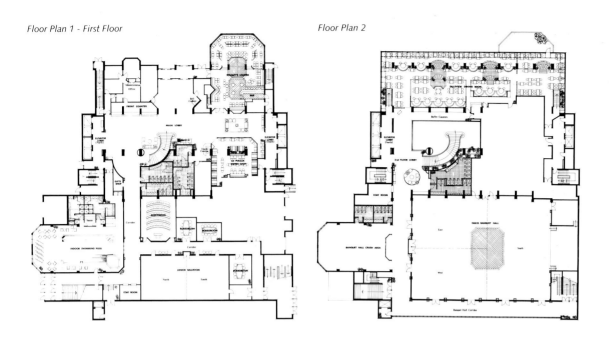

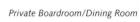
Private Boardroom/Dining Room

ALA MOANA HOTEL

HOPE ISLAND
RESORT

Logos were created for four hotels:
Ala Moana Hotel in Honolulu, Hawaii;
Hope Island Resort in Surfers Paradise, Australia;
Palau Pacific Resort in the Republic of Belau; and
LeLagon Pacific Resort in Port-Vila, Vanuatu.

palau pacific resort

PACIFIC RESORT
LE LAGON

DAI-ICHI HOTEL TOKYO BAY
Tokyo, Japan
Simple rosewood Chinese moldings and a color
palette of dark teal, dark mauve and black achieve
a contemporary oriental ambiance at the entrance
of the 100-seat Rogairo Restaurant.

MEDIA FIVE
A DESIGN CORPORATION
Media Five Plaza, 345 Queen Street, Honolulu, Hawaii 96813
808/524-2040, Fax: 808/538-1529

MEDIA FIVE

At Media Five, design is a total concept. For this reason, the firm offers a combination of services in architecture, interior design, graphic design, planning and programming. These services are provided separately, in combination or comprehensively according to a client's need for a strong, well-integrated project identity. ▭ Whether it's a destination resort, a private residence or a corporate office, every project is carefully designed to make an essential statement—one that is appropriate, special, and above all, personal. ▭ Since 1972, Media Five has evolved and grown according to a certain aspiration: to be the Pacific Basin's center for design. It has been building toward this goal on the strength of superior performance, the talent and teamwork of its people, and the trust it has won in the business of design.

SUNHILLS COUNTRY CLUB
Utsunomiya, Japan
The clubhouse and hotel is designed as a modified "L" connected by a projected half-circular form to command a 180-degree view of the golf course.

SUNHILLS COUNTRY CLUB
Utsunomiya, Japan
The focal point in this hotel is a polished brass and glass stairway beneath an oversized skylight.

MAUNA LANI BAY HOTEL AND BUNGALOWS
Kohala Coast of Hawaii
This award-winning bungalow offers guests luxurious amenities. Furnishings in koa wood and a neutral color palette complement the natural environment.

DAI-ICHI HOTEL TOKYO BAY
Tokyo, Japan
Standard guest rooms feature a European look with dark taupe walls and off-white trim. Furniture selection furthers the continental feeling with taupe and peach accents.

NEW OTANI KAIMANA BEACH HOTEL
Honolulu, Hawaii
For the renovation of this penthouse suite, an oriental theme was incorporated into the bath while taking advantage of spectacular views of Waikiki.

SEA RANCH COTTAGES
Maui, Hawaii

The exteriors of the cottages were designed to emulate the Hawaiian plantation lifestyle. From the lanais, guests have unobstructed views of the shoreline.

BELLEVIEW NAGAO RESORT
Gotemba, Japan

The design concept is that of a resort village, similar to the small towns found in mountainous areas of Japan. Featured are two golf courses, a clubhouse and residential areas.

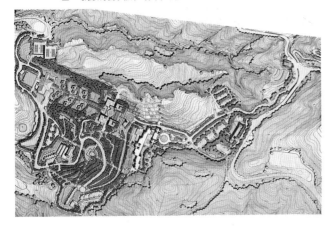

SHERATON FIJI
Nadi, Fiji

Tropical architectural elements found here during the British colonization were incorporated into the design. Wooden awnings, trellises and simple construction lines carry the theme throughout the grounds.

WYNDHAM GREENSPOINT HOTEL
Houston, Texas
*The contemporary registration desk
is located in the atrium.*

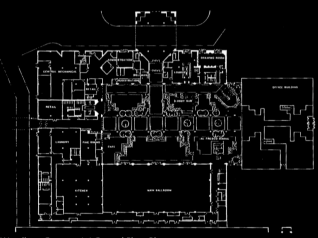

Wyndham Greenspoint Ground Floor Plan

WYNDHAM GREENSPOINT HOTEL
Houston, Texas
The elevator lobby is clad in marble.

MORRIS ☆ ARCHITECTS

3355 West Alabama	700 13th Street N.W.	Catalina Landing	201 North Magnolia Avenue
Suite 200	Suite 950	320 Golden Shore, Suite 340	Suite 100
Houston, Texas 77098	Washington, DC 20005	Long Beach, California 90802	Orlando, Florida 32801
713/622-1180. Fax: 713/622-7021	202/737-1180. Fax: 202/628-2256	310/437-7175. Fax: 310/437-1827	407/839-0414. Fax: 407/839-0410

MORRIS ☆ ARCHITECTS

Morris ☆ Architects has an excellent reputation in hospitality design not only in Houston but nationwide. During the past twenty years, the firm has been involved in the design or renovation of hotels totalling over 30,000 keys. ▭ The firm's most recent hospitality project opened on Valentine's day of this year as part of the University of Texas' M.D. Anderson Cancer Center. The Jesse H. Jones Rotary House is a full service, 200-room hotel with a special patient/guest relations program. Managed by Marriott, the hotel is intended as a "home away from home" for cancer patients and their families, often during extended stays. ▭ Established in 1938 the firm provides architectural design, interior architectural design, master planning and graphic design services not only for hospitality, but also for health care facilities, commercial buildings, retail and mixed-use developments, performing arts centers and libraries. The high percentage of major projects they have done for repeat clients attests to the quality of Morris ☆ Architects' work and the responsiveness of their staff.

WYNDHAM GREENSPOINT HOTEL
Houston, Texas
Located in a major suburban office

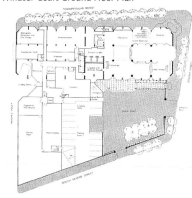

Windsor Court Ground Floor Plan

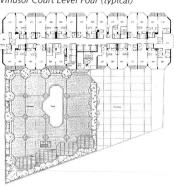

Windsor Court Level Four (typical)

WINDSOR COURT HOTEL
New Orleans, Louisiana
Located in the commercial district near the historic French Quarter in New Orleans, this facility is designed to be a "super-luxury" hotel for the top level business traveler.

WINDSOR COURT HOTEL
New Orleans, Louisiana
A variety of meeting rooms, including small private rooms, architecturally reinforces historic aspects of the French Quarter.

WINDSOR COURT HOTEL
New Orleans, Louisiana
The restaurant design provides an elegant atmosphere for fine dining.

Austin Guest Quarters Ground Floor

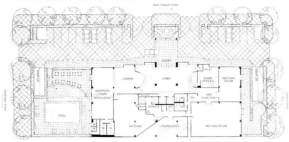

Austin Guest Quarters Second Floor Plan

GUEST QUARTERS AUSTIN
Austin, Texas
The main lobby utilizes natural wood paneling and flooring with marble casements for the elevator doors.

GUEST QUARTERS AUSTIN
Austin, Texas
The upper floors of this 193-suite hotel step back to create roof terraces that offer a view of the Texas State Capitol and the hill country.

GUEST QUARTERS AUSTIN
Austin, Texas
The "15th Street Cafe" is a versatile space which can function as a dining or gathering space.

Game Room
The Game Room features a pool table, bar, books, T.V. and games. The back windowed wall focuses on the lakefront.

ONE DESIGN CENTER, INC.

2828 Lawndale Drive, P.O. Box 29426, Greensboro, North Carolina 27429
919/288-0134, Fax: 919/282-7369

ONE DESIGN CENTER, INC.

Founded in 1973 by Cynthia Folds and Linda Higgins, One Design Center, Inc., has extensive experience in a wide range of commercial interiors; and specializes in hotels, restaurants and private clubs. For seven consecutive years, the firm has been ranked one of the top interior design firms for the hospitality industry by *Interior Design* magazine. ☐☐☐ Known for reliability, professionalism, and ability to create superb, innovative interiors, the firm has established long-term relationships with a broad spectrum of clients. Each client is assured creative and technical excellence, with attention to critical deadlines and details. ☐☐☐ Throughout the east and midwest, One Design Center has left its mark on the interiors of many hospitality properties and made an impression on clients as well—by producing aesthetic, functional interior design. One of their premier projects is the Uwharrie Point Lodge located at Badin Lake in North Carolina, the company's home state. The lodge is surrounded by a championship golf course overlooking a 5300-acre lake. The adjoining Uwharrie National Forest provides natural beauty to set the theme for this exclusive, lakefront retreat.

UWHARRIE POINT LODGE
Badin Lake, North Carolina
Exterior from Lake
Southern design is repeated on the back exterior of the lodge providing a relaxing lakeside environment.

Exterior - front
The Southern traditional design draws upon the heritage of hospitality and charm associated with this area.

Architect: Small Kane Architects PA

Main Building–First Floor

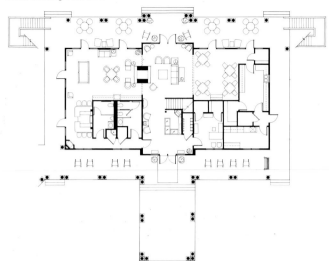

Main Building–Second Floor

Living Room
An eclectic mix of furnishings, non-traditional fabrics, and local crafts create an inviting and relaxing atmosphere.

Guest Wing

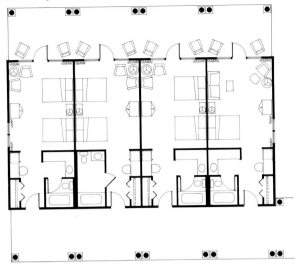

Bar
Materials and furnishings were used throughout to relate to the exterior.

Dining Room
Architectural detailing and judicious selections of furnishings, finishes and accessories create an impression of stability. Interiors were also designed to be cost-efficient and easily maintainable.

Guest Room
Each room has a balcony overlooking the lake. Rooms are individualized by art and accessories, and appropriately named so that guests can request their favorites.

DOUBLETREE INN AT THE COLONNADE
Balitmore, Maryland
*Flame maple paneling and silk wallcovering was
inspired by the Swedish beidemeier sofa. Lobby is
further defined by octagonal area rug and circular
ceiling coffer opening up to a trompe l'oeil sky.*

DOUBLETREE INN AT THE COLONNADE
Balitmore, Maryland
*The Polo Grill features a compact bar entrance
opening onto a multi-level dining area. Dimmable
ambient cove lighting creates changing levels of
illumination in the windowless space.*

DOUBLETREE INN AT THE COLONNADE
Balitmore, Maryland
*Wood panel details flow around the granite capped
registration desk. Etched bronze
elevator door panels repeat the elliptical motif.*

RITA ST. CLAIR ASSOCIATES INC.

1009 North Charles Street, Baltimore, Maryland 21201-5493

410 752-1313 Fax: 410 752-1335

WASHINGTON FIRENZE PIETRA SANTA

130

RITA ST.CLAIR ASSOCIATES, INC.

Rita St.Clair Associates, Inc. uses a unique combination of classical and modern design elements with the state-of-the-art technology necessary for the operation of contemporary hospitality facilities. ▭ Consumer-driven designs are inspired by the geographic location of each project. Visual regional flavor instills a "personality" that creates a comforting sense of place for guests. ▭ Ms. St.Clair believes that the most successful interiors must be designed for both the operator and the user's needs. Functional and cost-effective benefits are the result of unique aesthetic solutions. The outcome is a distinctive, expressive interior ambiance which fulfills the expectations of all. ▭ Rita St.Clair, FASID, a member of the Interior Design Hall of Fame, is also a syndicated columnist, and founder and president of her namesake firm which has provided space planning, interior architectural design, and purchasing services for over thirty years.

HOTEL INTERCONTINENTAL MIAMI
Miami, Florida
Palm Court Restaurant
The elevated gazebo-like room is enhanced by a lattice enclosure that screens surrounding lobby activities. Cove lighting illuminates the artist mural within the coffered ceiling.

THE OCTAGON
U.S.F.&G. Mt. Washington Campus
Baltimore, Maryland
Recreation of a Victorian resort hotel within a circa 1855 historic shell. New designs for decorative elements of handcrafted glass, tiles and millwork within the central atrium frame a view of an artist mural in the reception room.

THE OCTAGON
U.S.F.&G. Mt. Washington Campus
Baltimore, Maryland
Each guest room is uniquely treated to its own color scheme of hand-glazed walls, softgoods, and imported furniture and art.

Photographer: Mick Hales

THE PALMER HOUSE HILTON
Chicago, Illinois
Red Lacquer Room
Red luminous wall glazing adds drama to this room with gilded panel moldings. The cream and gilt cove and ceiling and gold draperies impart elegance and freshness in contrast to the rich palette.

Photographer: Wayne Cable

HOTEL INTERCONTINENTAL MIAMI
Miami, Florida
Lobby
The massive travertine atrium lobby becomes festive with overscaled umbrellas set aglow by filtered spotlights. Triangular area rugs anchor groupings of painted rattan lounge furniture gathered around the Henry Moore sculpture.

THE PALMER HOUSE HILTON
Chicago, Illinois
This bronze and etched glass escalator enclosure is located in the street level vestibule and heralds the entrance to the lower level restaurant.

Photographer: Wayne Cable

Photographer: Dan Forer

THE PALMER HOUSE HILTON
Chicago, Illinois
Garden murals by artist, Joseph Sheppard, fill architectural niches and create a pavilion-like effect for the State Ballroom. Faux marble pilasters and glazed finishes delineate the ornate moldings.

Photographer: Wayne Cable

133

WASHINGTON COURT HOTEL
Washington, DC
Presidential Suite
Vignette of sitting area
overlooking Capitol Hill

WASHINGTON COURT HOTEL
Washington, DC
Presidential Suite
Complete furnishings and
fixtures renovation working
with existing structure.

THE H. CHAMBERS COMPANY

THE H. CHAMBERS COMPANY
1010 North Charles Street, Baltimore Maryland 21201
410/727-4535 Fax: 410/727-6982

HOUSE AND GARDEN, LTD.
10 Lyford Cay Shopping Center, Nassau, Bahamas
809/362-4140 Fax: 809/362-4828

THE H. CHAMBERS COMPANY

The H. Chambers Company, established 1899, played a major role in the development of the new, emerging profession known as interior design. Their growth and reputation in the field resulted from a professional approach to design and the human environment and their concern for quality workmanship and staffing by only the most qualified designers. During the 1940's, when the hospitality industry began to appraise the effectual value of planned interior space, their expanded services were increasingly utilized for hotels, inns and clubs. It is from these beginnings that they have carefully developed the full service design company that they are today. ▭ The size and quality of their staff allows them to render a variety of professional design services including space planning, architectural interiors, interior design, and the complete spectrum of specifications for furnishings, purchasing and expediting, warehousing, delivery and installation, as well as project supervision and management.

EDISON HOTEL
New York, New York
Historically renovated Lobby/Reception area of 1910 hotel, restored as part of Times Square revitalization.

■ **PLAZA SUITE HOTEL**
Seacaucus, New Jersey
Entry to Cocktail Lounge

■ **FOREST LAKE CLUB**
Columbia, South Carolina
Ballroom (total renovation)

■ **SHERATON INNER**
HARBOR HOTEL
Baltimore, Maryland
Executive Suite
(total renovation)

Photographer: Whitney Cox

GRAYSON'S RESTAURANT
Germantown, Maryland
Main Entrance

GRAYSON'S RESTAURANT
Germantown, Maryland
Bar area

Photographer: Whitney Cox

Photographer: Whitney Cox

GRAYSON'S RESTAURANT
Germantown, Maryland
Total renovation of existing restaurant.

Photographer: Whitney Cox

**THE HYATT
ATLANTA AIRPORT
College Park, Georgia**
*This hotel was converted from
a Holiday Inn. Eclectic and
whimsical design elements
create the drama of the
Main Lobby.*

**THE HYATT
REGENCY WOODFIELD
Schaumburg, Illinois**
*Netti's Bar, a contemporary
Chicago speakeasy.*

URBAN WEST LTD

685 West Ohio at Union, Chicago, Illinois 60610
312/733-4111, Fax: 312/733-4761
CHICAGO · MIAMI · LOS ANGELES · SAN FRANCISCO

URBAN WEST

Urban West is a multi-disciplined, highly conceptual organization formed to address hotel design from a broader, more informed, and more creative approach than the traditional status quo. The firm is composed of architects, interior designers, graphic designers, and hotel operations people to create a team that can intelligently address the complex issues inherent in contemporary hotel design.   The most important component of their work is the creation of "highest value" for a given budget and set of objectives. The firm's projects have consistently been the most operationally and financially successful in their marketplace, largly due to the optimum design strategy and execution which they have wrought. Rather than duplicating other successful projects, they enjoy the creation of design "originals," which often become new genres in themselves. They apply a strong sensitivity to environment, existing architecture, venue, and clientele in completing the design. The final project is great theater; the guest enjoys an experience that is strongly positive and decidedly memorable.

THE AMWAY GRAND PLAZA
Grand Rapids, Michigan
View through "A" Suite dining room bay window to Grand River.

THE AMWAY GRAND PLAZA
Grand Rapids, Michigan
Overall lobby view of Pantlind Building depicting the 1913 era.

139

THE BELDEN STRATFORD
Chicago, Illinois
**I.A.H.A.M.A. Gold Key
Award Winner, 1991**
*Lobby view showing Second
Empire detail*

THE AMWAY GRAND PLAZA
Grand Rapids, Michigan
*The "1913" Room Restaurant whose
design elements are derived from
the era in which the hotel was built.*

THE AMWAY GRAND PLAZA
Grand Rapids, Michigan
*Entryway to "A" Suite where former guests have included
Margaret Thatcher, Gerald Ford and Ronald Reagan.*

THE AMWAY GRAND PLAZA
Grand Rapids, Michigan
Typical king guest room in Pantlind Building with view towards seating area.

THE AMWAY GRAND PLAZA
Grand Rapids, Michigan
Typical double-double guest room in new tower contrasts traditional and contemporary elements.

THE AMWAY GRAND PLAZA
Grand Rapids, Michigan
View through indigenous Michigan landscape to Garden Court Lounge porch.

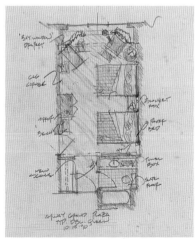

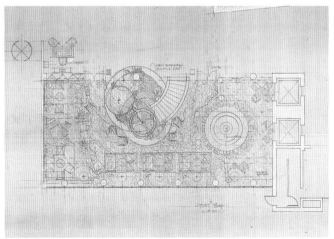

Amway Grand Plaza–Garden Court Floor Plan

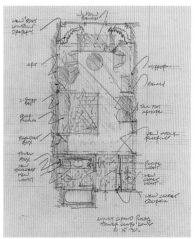

Amway Grand Plaza–Typical Tower Room

Amway Grand Plaza–Typical Double Queen

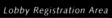

Lobby Registration Area

Lobby Furniture Plan

Lobby and Lobby Lounge

VICTOR HUFF PARTNERSHIP

250 Albion Street, Denver, Colorado 80220
303/388-9140

VICTOR HUFF PARTNERSHIP

"Designing for Guest Satisfaction" brings the greatest operational efficiencies and property profits. Whether they are designing hotels, resorts, casinos, clubs, assisted living facilities or restaurants, the firm's versatility enables clients to meet the demands of their targeted market. Tough times create "windows of opportunity" for the professional firm that has the dedication, innovation, flexibility and versatility to offer value, client-driven service and technical excellence. With the support of industry working relationships, they develop the best team for any project, whether it is complex or straightforward, new construction or renovation.

SOCIETY CENTER
MARRIOTT
Cleveland, Ohio
Executive Board Room

Restaurant Seating Plan

Bar/Lounge Furniture Plan

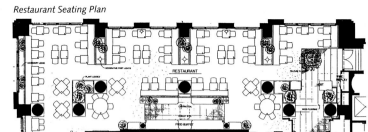

Lounge

Restaurant–Main Dining Room

Presidential Suite

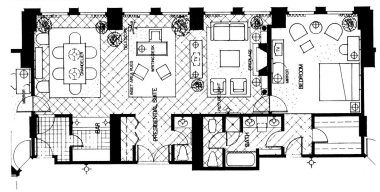

▮ *Presidential Suite
Overlooking Lake Erie*

▮ *Adjoining Bedroom of
Presidential Suite*

▮ *Living Room of Presidential Suite*

DOUBLETREE HOTEL/PARK WEST
Dallas, Texas
Lobby Bar

VIVIAN|NICHOLS ASSOCIATES INC.

Suite 302. LB 105. 2811 McKinney Avenue. Dallas. Texas 75204

214 979-9050. Fax: 214 979-9053

VIVIAN|NICHOLS ASSOCIATES, INC.

V|N Associates, Inc., founded in 1985 by partners Dierdre Vivian and Reggi Nichols-Hales, specializes in interior architecture and design for the hospitality industry. The firm approaches design in a way that successfully melds client and market needs with that of the hotel guest and the demands set by the property and location. ▭ The entire firm is dedicated to design; and approach their respected professions as careers. They insist on the betterment of each project and have a genuine concern for its success. Along with their dedication comes a sense of pride and integrity to design only the very best within budget guidelines for all projects both large and small. V|N Associates, Inc. is a young, dynamic, energetic firm whose work has earned national awards and recognition.

DOUBLETREE HOTEL/ PARK WEST
Dallas, Texas
Loggia

HYATT REGENCY SUITES
Chicago, Illinois
Executive Board Room

WESTCHASE HILTON HOTEL
Houston, Texas
Typical Guestroom

HYATT REGENCY SUITES
Chicago, Illinois
Typical Guest Suite

WATERFRONT CENTRE HOTEL
Vancouver, British Columbia
Restaurant Entry

WATERFRONT CENTRE HOTEL
Vancouver, British Columbia
Lobby

WATERFRONT CENTRE HOTEL
Vancouver, British Columbia
Prefunction Corridor

WILSON & ASSOCIATES

3811 Turtle Creek Boulevard
Dallas, Texas 75219
214/521-6753, Fax 214/521-0207

415 East 54th Street, Suite 15D
New York, New York 10022
212/319-0898, Fax 212/486-9729

8342 1/2 Melrose Avenue
Los Angeles, California 90069
213/651-3234, Fax 213/852-4758

84A/86A Tanjong Pagar Road
Singapore 0208
65-227-1151, Fax 65-227-6124

P.O. Box 1216
Sunninghill 2157, South Africa
011/884-7040, Fax 011/884-7062

WILSON & ASSOCIATES

Specializing in interior architectural design. Wilson & Associates was founded in 1975 and incorporated in 1978 by current President. Trisha Wilson. ▭ To date. the firm has designed and installed more than 35,000 guestrooms in over 70 hotels world-wide. Wilson & Associates offers the full range of interior architectural design services from initial space planning and design through construction documents and administration. Further. they offer additional services such as graphics signage and procurement. ▭ Consistently named among the top three interior design firms in the country by industry professionals. Wilson & Associates receives top honors annually in design competitions for both new construction and historical renovation. For four consecutive years, the firm has been chosen by industry peers as most respected for work in the field of hospitality design; is a five-time winner of the prestigious American Hotel and Motel Association's Gold Key Award for excellence in hotel design; and has taken top honors five consecutive years in *Lodging Hospitality's* Designer Circle Awards Program. ▭ Its design practice integrates the skills of architects and interior designers to offer clients the full scope of services from design concept through installation. With a staff of more than 80 professionals including registered architects, accredited designers, design assistants and administrative staff, the firm attributes its success to the diverse capabilities and experience of its professionals.

INN OF THE ANASAZI
Santa Fe, New Mexico
59 room 5-star Inn
Living Room

INN OF THE ANASAZI
Santa Fe, New Mexico
Guestroom Corridor

INN OF THE ANASAZI
Santa Fe, New Mexico
Exterior of Inn

INN OF THE ANASAZI
Santa Fe, New Mexico
Living Room From Corridor

INN OF THE ANASAZI
Santa Fe, New Mexico
Guestroom

INN OF THE ANASAZI
Santa Fe, New Mexico
Restaurant

INN OF THE ANASAZI
Santa Fe, New Mexico
Vignette off lobby

WATERFRONT CENTRE HOTEL
Vancouver, British Columbia
490 room business/tourist hotel
Ballroom Prefunction

WATERFRONT CENTRE HOTEL
Vancouver, British Columbia
Specialty Restaurant

WATERFRONT CENTRE HOTEL
Vancouver, British Columbia
Lobby Seating

WATERFRONT CENTRE HOTEL
Vancouver, British Columbia
Lobby Lounge

153

AiGROUP/ARCHITECTS, P.C.
1197 Peachtree Street
Atlanta, Georgia 30361
404/873-2555

AIELLO ASSOCIATES, INC.
1443 Wazee Street
Denver, Colorado 80202-1309
303/892-7024
Fax: 303/892-7039

BARRY DESIGN ASSOCIATES, INC.
11601 Wilshire Boulevard
Suite 102
Los Angeles, California 90025
310/478 6081
Fax: 310/312 9926

BLAIR SPANGLER INTERIOR AND
GRAPHIC DESIGN, INCORPORATED
2789 25th Street
San Francisco, California 94110
415/285-8034
Fax: 415/285-4651

BRASELLE DESIGN COMPANY
423 Thirty-First Street
Newport Beach, California 92663
714/673-6522
Fax: 714/673-2461

BRENNAN BEER GORMAN/
ARCHITECTS
BRENNAN BEER GORMAN MONK/
INTERIORS
515 Madison Avenue
New York, New York, 10022
212/888-7663
Fax: 212/935-3868

1155 21st Street NW
Washington D.C. 20036
202/452-1644
Fax: 202/452-1647

19/F Queen's Place
74 Queen's Road
Central Hong Kong
852/525-9766
Fax:852/525-9850

CAROLE KORN INTERIORS, INC.
825 South Bayshore Drive
Miami, Florida 33131
305/375-8080
Fax: 305/374-5522

COLE MARTINEZ CURTIS
AND ASSOCIATES
308 Washington Boulevard
Marina del Rey, California 90292
310/827-7200
Fax: 310/822-5803

CONCEPTS 4, INC.
300 North Continental
Suite 320
El Segundo, California 90245
310/640-0290
Fax: 310/640-0009

DESIGN 1 INTERIORS
2049 Century Park East
Suite 3000
Los Angeles, California 90067
310/553-5032
Fax: 310/785-0445

DESIGN CONTINUUM, INC.
Five Piedmont Center
Suite 300
Atlanta, Georgia 30305
404/266-0095
Fax: 404/266-8252

DI LEONARDO INTERNATIONAL, INC.
2350 Post Road
Suite 1
Warwick, Rhode Island 02886-2242
401/732-2900
Fax. 401/732-5315

The Centre Mark Building, Room 608
287-289 Queen's Road
Central, Hong Kong
852/851-7282, 851-7227
Fax. 852/851-7287

DIANNE JOYCE DESIGN GROUP, INC.
2675 South Bayshore Drive
Miami, Florida 33133
305/858-8895
Fax: 305/858-4544

DOW/FLETCHER
127 Bellevue Way SE
Suite 100
Bellevue, Washington 98004
206/454-0029
Fax: 206/646-5904

HAROLD THOMPSON & ASSOCIATES
15260 Ventura Boulevard
Suite 1910
Sherman Oaks, California 91403
818/789-3005
Fax: 818/789-3089

HIRSCH/BEDNER ASSOCIATES
3216 Nebraska Avenue
Santa Monica, California 90404
310/829-9087
Fax 310/453-1182

49 Wellington Street
London, England WC2E 7BN
071/240-2099
Fax 071/240-2050

4/F Kai Tak Commercial Building
317-321 Des Voeux Road
Central Hong Kong
852/542-2022
Fax 852/545-2051

11 Stamford Road
#02-08 Capitol Building
Singapore 0617
65-337-2511, Fax 65-337-2460

909 W. Peachtree Street, N.E.
Atlanta, Georgia
404/873-4379
Fax 404/872-3588

HOCHHEISER-ELIAS DESIGN
GROUP, INC.
226 East 54th Street
New York, New York 10022
212/826-8700
Fax: 212/826-8703

HOWARD-LUACES & ASSOCIATES
5785 Sunset Drive
South Miami, Florida 33143
305/662-9002
Fax: 305/662-7006

JAMES NORTHCUTT ASSOCIATES
717 North La Cienega Boulevard
Los Angeles, California 90069
310/659-8595
Fax: 310/659-7120

JOHN PORTMAN & ASSOCIATES
ARCHITECTS AND ENGINEERS
231 Peachtree Street, NE, Suite 200
Atlanta, Georgia 30303
404/614-5252
Fax: 404/614-5553

JOSZI MESKAN ASSOCIATES
INTERIOR ARCHITECTURE
AND DESIGN
479 Ninth Street
San Francisco, California 94103
415/431-0500
Fax: 415/431-9339

LYNN WILSON ASSOCIATES
INTERNATIONAL
116 Anhambra Circle
Coral Gables, Florida 33134
305/442-4041
Fax: 305/443-4276

11620 Wilshire Boulevard, Suite 350
Los Angeles, California 90025
310/854-1141
Fax: 310/854-1149

MDI INTERNATIONAL INC.
DESIGN CONSULTANTS
4 Wellington Street East
Fourth Floor
Toronto, Ontario, Canada
M5E 1C5
416/369-0123
Fax: 416/369-0998

Europe/Middle East
74A Kensington Park Road
London, England W11 2LP
4471 727-5683
Fax: 4471 229-2314

Asia/Pacific Rim
11-15 Wing Wo Street Room 501
Wo Hing Commercial Building
Central Hong Kong
852/815-2325
Fax: 852/544-5412

Caribbean/South America
3 Frederick Street, Port of Spain
Trinidad W.I.
809/624-4430
Fax: 809/623-1217

MEDIA FIVE
A DESIGN CORPORATION
Media Five Plaza
345 Queen Street
Honolulu, Hawaii 96813
808/524-2040
Fax: 808/538-1529

MORRIS ARCHITECTS
3355 West Alabama
Suite 200
Houston, Texas 77098
713/622-1180
Fax: 713/662-7021

700 13th Street N.W.
Suite 950
Washington, DC 20005
202/737-1180
Fax: 202/628-2256

Catalina Landing
320 Golden Shore
Suite 340
Long Beach, California 90802
310/437-7175
Fax: 310/437-1827

201 North Magnolia Avenue
Suite 100
Orlando, Florida 32801
407/839-0414
Fax: 407/839-0410

ONE DESIGN CENTER, INC.
2828 Lawndale Drive
Greensboro, North Carolina 27408
919/288-0134
Fax: 919/282-7369

PACIFIC DESIGN GROUP
Australia
Sydney:
343 Pacific Highway
CROWS NEST NSW 2065
612/929-0922
Fax: 612/923-2558

Gold Coast:
Suite 7 2-4 Elliot Street
Bundall QLD 4217
075/38-4499
Fax 075/38-3847

Jakarta:
Suite 1603, Wisma Antara
JL. Medan Merdeka Selatan 17
Jakarta 10110 Indonesia
6221/384-3880
Fax: 6221/384-5329

Hong Kong:
1701 Hennessy House
313 Hennessy Road
Wanchai, Hong Kong
852/834-7404
Fax: 852/834-5675

PACIFIC DESIGN GROUP (cont.)
Fiji:
PO Box 14465
73 Gordon Street
Suva
679/303-858
Fax: 679/303-868

RITA ST. CLAIR ASSOCIATES, INC.
1009 North Charles Street
Baltimore, Maryland 21201-5493
410/752-1313
Fax: 410/752-1335

TEXEIRA, INC.
11811 Bellagio Road
Los Angeles, California 90049
310/471-2355
Fax: 310/440-2149

THE H. CHAMBERS COMPANY
1010 North Charles Street
Baltimore Maryland 21201
410/727-4535
Fax: 410/727-6982

House and Garden, Ltd.
10 Lyford Cay Shopping Center
Nassau, Bahamas
809/362-4140
Fax: 809/362-4828

URBAN WEST, LTD.
685 West Ohio at Union
Chicago, Illinois 60610
312/733-4111
Fax: 312/733-4761

VICTOR HUFF PARTNERSHIP
250 Albion Street
Denver, Colorado 80220
303/388-9140

VIVIAN/NICHOLS ASSOCIATES, INC.
Suite 302, LB 105
2811 McKinney Avenue
Dallas, Texas 75204
214/979-9050
Fax: 214/979-9053

WILSON & ASSOCIATES
3811 Turtle Creek Boulevard
Dallas, Texas 75219
214/521-6753
Fax 214/521-0207

415 East 54th Street, Suite 15D
New York, New York 10022
212/319-0898
Fax 212/486-9729

8342 ½ Melrose Avenue
Los Angeles, California 90069
213/651-3234
Fax 213/852-4758

84A/86A Tanjong Pagar Road
Singapore 0208
65-227-1151
Fax 65-227-6124

P.O. Box 1216
Sunninghill 2157, South Africa
011/884-7040
Fax 011/884-7062

WIMBERLY ALLISON TONG & GOO
ARCHITECTS AND PLANNERS
2222 Kalakaua Avenue
Penthouse
Honolulu, Hawaii 96815
808/922-1253
Fax: 808/922-1250

2260 University Drive
Newport Beach, California 92660
714/574-8500
Fax: 714/574-8550

51 Neil Road, #02-20
Singapore 0208
65/227-2618
Fax: 65/227-0650

Second Floor, Waldron House
57 Old Church Street
London SW3 5BS, England
071/376-3260
Fax: 071/376-3193

Africa
Bophuthatswana,
  The Palace of the Lost City

Australia
Cairns
  Plaza Hotel and The Pier
  Ramada Reef Resort

Melbourne
  Bryson Hotel
  Hilton Hotel

Sydney
  Capital Hotel,
  Hilton Hotel
  Radisson Century Hotel

Canada
British Columbia, Vancouver
  Waterfront Center Hotel
Niagara Falls
  Sheraton Fallsview

Caribbean Islands
Aruba
  unidentified

China
Shanghai
  Shanghai Centre

Cook Islands
Sheraton Cook Islands

Fiji
Nadi
  Sheraton Fiji

France
Deauville
  unidentified

Hong Kong
Deep Water Bay
  Hong Kong Country Club
Kowloon
  The New World Hotel

Indonesia
Bali
  Grand Hyatt Bali

Japan
Gotemba
  Belleview Nagao Resort
Okinawa
  unidentified
Tokyo Bay
  Dai-ichi Hotel
Tokyo
  Four Seasons Chinzan-so

Utsunomiya
  Sunhills Country Club

Mexico
Acapulco
  The Villa Vera Hotel and Racquet Club
Monterrey
  Las Misiones Golf and Country Club

Micronesia
Saipan
  Plumeria Resort

Netherlands Antilles
St. Maarten
  Port De Plaisnce

New Zealand
Auckland
  Auckland Club
Christchurch
  Noah's Hotel

Singapore
Shangri-La Hotel

South Korea
Pusan
  Paradise Beach Hotel

Spain
Los Millares Golf and Country Club

Tahiti
Bora Bora
  The Hotel Bora Bora

Taiwan
Taipei
  The Sherwood Taipei

Thailand
Bangkok
  The Peninsula Bangkok

United Arab Emeriates
Dubai
  The Royal Abjar Hotel

United States of America

Alaska
Anchorage
  West Coast International Inn

Arizona
Scottsdale
  Sheraton Scottsdale
Tuscon
  Radisson Hotel

California
Anaheim
  The Sheraton Anaheim Hotel
Beverly Hills
  The Peninsula Beverly Hills Hotel
Coronado
  Loews Coronado Bay
Fallbrook
  Pala Mesa Resort
Huntington Beach
  Hilton Waterfront
Indian Wells
  Hotel Indian Wells
Laguna Beach
  Surf and Sand
Los Angeles
  The Century Plaza Hotel
  Hotel Bel Air
  Hyatt Regency Lax
  Inter-Continental
  The Wilshire
Newport Beach
  Four Seasons Hotel
  Sheraton Newport
Palm Desert
  Bighorn Country Club
Pasadena
  The Ritz-Carlton Huntington Hotel
Rancho Mirage
  Westin Mission Hills Resort
Redondo Beach
  Portofino Inn At The Marina
San Francisco
  Hyatt Fisherman's Wharf Hotel
  The Pan Pacific San Francisco
  unidentified

Colorado
Castle Rock
  Castle Pines Golf Club
Central City
  Bullwhackers Gaming Establishment
Denver
  Embassy Suites,
  Westin Hotel Tabor Center
Telluride
  Doral Telluride
Vail
  The Vail Athletic Club

Delaware
Wilmington
  Dupont Hotel

Florida
Bal Harbour
  Sheraton Bal Harbour
Coral Gables
  Colonnade Hotel
  Hyatt
Fisher Island
  Fisher Island Clubhouse

Coconut Grove
  Grand Bay

Fort Lauderdale
  Sheraton Suites Plantation
  Westin
Key West
  Hyatt

Miami
  Hotel Intercontinental
  Turnberry Isle Hotel
  Williams Island
Orlando
  Disney's Yacht Club Resort
  Disney's Port Orleans Resort
    Disney World
  Disney's Vaction Club Resort
  The Grand Floridian Beach Resort
    Disney World
Palm Beach
  The Ocean Grand Hotel
St. Petersburg
  Don Ce Sar
West Palm Beach
  Palm Beach Airport Hilton

Georgia
Atlanta
  Hotel Nikko,
  J. W. Marriott
  The Suite Hotel Underground Atlanta
College Park
  The Hyatt Atlanta Airport

Hawaii
Honolulu
  Hilton Hawaiian Village
  New Otani Kaimana Beach Hotel
Kauai, Poipu, Kauai
  Hyatt Regency
Kohala Coast
  Mauna Lani Bay Hotel and Bungalows
Lanai
  Lodge at Koele
Maui
  Grand Hyatt Wailea
  Sea Ranch Cottages
  Stoffer Wailes
  Unidentified

Illinois
Chicago
  The Balden Stratford
  Hyatt Regency Suites
  Inter-Continental
  The Palmer House Hilton
Schaumburg
  The Hyatt Regency Wood Field

Maryland
Baltimore
  Doubletree Inn At The Colonnade
  Harbor Court Hotel
  Sheraton Inner Harbor Hotel
  The Octogon U.S.F.& G. Mt.
    Washington Campus
Germantown
  Grayson's Restaurant

Michigan
Grand Rapids
  The Amway Grand Plaza
Kalamazoo
  Radison Plaza Hotel Kalamazoo Center

Louisiana
New Orleans
  Windsor Court Hotel

New Jersey
Seacaucus
  Plaza Suite Hotel

New Mexico
Santa Fe
  Inn of the Anasazi

New York
New York City
  Edison Hotel
  The Peninsula Hotel
  Grand Bay
  The Ramada Renaissance Hotel-Times
    Square
  Sherry Netherland
  The Sheraton Manhattan Hotel

North Carolina
Ashville
  Grove Park Inn
Badin Lake
  Uwharrie Point Lodge
Raleigh
  Washington Duke Inn and Golf Club

Ohio
Cleveland
  Cleveland Society Center Marriott

Pennsylvania
Philadelphia
  The Rittenhouse Hotel

South Carolina
Columbia
  Forest Lake Club

Texas
Austin
  Guest Quarters Austin

Dallas
  Doubletree Hotel/Park West
Houston
  Westchase Hilton Hotel
  Wyndham Greenspoint
San Antonio
  HotelFairmount

Virginia
Richmond
  The Jefferson Hotel
  The Richmond Airport Hilton

Washington
Everett
  Everett Quality Inn
Kirkland
  Woodmark Hotel
Leavenworth
  Best Western Icicle Inn
Seattle
  Seattle Ramada Hotel
Wenatchee
  West Coast Wenatchee Center Hotel

Washington, DC
  Courtyard By Marriott
  The Sheraton Carlton
  Washington Court Hotel

Yugoslavia
Belgrade
  unidentified